If ever there is a time when we need help with new ways to care for and encourage young people in their faith journey, it is now. From the deep dive into the latest research to broad-based applications, Sticky Faith Innovation *is not a cookie-cutter quick fix, but offers a solid and proven way of taking teenagers' faith and life seriously, and guiding you through a process to help you get there. You won't find a more helpful or empowering book for your team.*

—**Dr. Chap Clark**, author, *Sticky Faith* and *Hurt 2.0: Inside the World of Today's Teenagers*

With so much change in our world, we need leaders who are compassionate, creative, and courageous, willing to envision a preferred future with teenagers. Everyone who seeks to design that youth ministry vision needs a faithful and proven guide for the journey. Sticky Faith Innovation *is that guide that can get you "from here to there."*

—**April L. Diaz**, author, *Redefining the Role of a Youth Worker*

Teenagers need youth leaders who are filled with compassion and empathy to understand the changing world they're growing up in. And we youth leaders must, more than ever, tap into our creativity and courage to take big swings for our youth ministries to reach them. This is the book to set you on that journey. I'm in.

—**Josh Griffin**, co-founder, Download Youth Ministry

The Sticky Faith Innovation *process has allowed us to dream and make those dreams a reality in our ministry. Now, we are continually reimagining how to creatively serve our young people.*

—**Brad Hauge**, Director of Student Ministries, First Presbyterian Church, Spokane, WA

Fuller Youth Institute has done it again! Ministry leaders interested in the changing face of youth ministry will want to read this compelling, creative, and convicting guide on ways to invite youth and adults alike to rethink how they walk alongside teenagers exploring identity, belonging, and purpose. Grounded in solid research and deep learning, Sticky Faith Innovation *introduces a process that beckons youth ministry leaders to innovate. This book offers new insights that help youth ministry leaders grow in compassion for our young people even as we ourselves are transformed by our relationship with them.*

—**Dr. Sarah F. Farmer**, co-author, *Raising Hope: Four Pathways to Courageous Living for Black Youth*; General Editor, *Joy: A Guide for Youth Ministry*

Through compelling stories, practical steps, and scriptural grounding, Sticky Faith Innovation *will coach your team through the innovation process and inspire you to experiment in your ministry in ways that leave it—and you—changed.*

—**Jen Bradbury**, author and Minister of Youth and Family, Lutheran Church of the Atonement, Barrington, IL

I don't know of many resources like this that are theologically-grounded, research-based, and at the same time both accessible and contextually applicable across denominations, congregation sizes, budgets, and resources. Reading this made me excited for the future of ministry as a whole and encouraged me to continue innovating in my context.

—**Kyle Lake**, High School and Family Life Director, Mars Hill Bible Church, Grandville, MI

Sticky Faith Innovation

STICKY FAITH
INNOVATION

How Your Compassion, Creativity, and Courage
Can Support Teenagers' Lasting Faith

STEVEN ARGUE & CALEB ROOSE

FULLER YOUTH INSTITUTE

Sticky Faith Innovation:
How Your Compassion, Creativity, and Courage
Can Support Teenagers' Lasting Faith

Foreword by Kara Powell and Brad Griffin
Cover and Interior Design: Katherine Botts Whitaker
Copy Editor: Joy Netanya Thompson
Editor: Rachel Dodd
Senior Editor: Brad M. Griffin

Published in the United States of America by
Fuller Youth Institute, 135 N. Oakland Ave., Pasadena, CA, 91182
fulleryouthinstitute.org

ISBN 978-0-9914880-8-7

Unless otherwise noted, all Scripture quotations are taken from
THE HOLY BIBLE, NEW INTERNATIONAL VERSION®, NIV® Copyright © 1973,
1978, 1984, 2011 by Biblica, Inc.® All rights reserved.

Scripture quotations marked MSG are taken from THE MESSAGE, copyright
© 1993, 2002, 2018 by Eugene H. Peterson. Used by permission of
NavPress. All rights reserved. Represented by Tyndale House Publishers, a
Division of Tyndale House Ministries.

Printed in the United States of America

To youth leaders.
Thank you for showing up
where young people need you most.
Your compassion moves us.
Your creativity inspires us.
Your courage motivates us.

Keep going.
We are with you and for you.

TABLE OF CONTENTS

FOREWORD
Kara Powell & Brad Griffin

Youth leaders, we believe in you. That optimistic conviction compelled us to start this Sticky Faith Innovation project five years ago.

But we also anticipated a few common villains that would make it tough for us to share what we learned with the world. You know the villains we're talking about:

Complacency.

Avoidance.

Resistance to change.

We were concerned we might have to work *really* hard to convince a lot of leaders that innovation was needed in youth ministry. We worried that the lure of ministry-as-usual would be too strong for many leaders to get motivated to change. (Not you, of course, but those others who are pretty comfortable with familiar youth ministry rhythms.)

Okay, if we're honest, we had those concerns because we feel the same temptations. We like normal. We thrive on predictability. And we've done more than our share of ministry-as-usual.

Enter a pandemic. Layer in explosive racial injustice and economic collapse.

Global events in 2020 (and their aftershocks) catapulted all of us into completely different orbits. Ministry—along with every other area of life—changed radically. While for months we hoped to get back to "normal," eventually we began to accept that instead we'd have to discover a "new normal."

So much for our worries about ministries stuck in complacency. Today's world requires us to change. While this was true before the pandemic, it has become even more evident.

Youth ministry has a long history of responding creatively to young people's needs. We've seen it through so many expressions of church and parachurch ministries across the decades—and many of us serve in ministry today because of the creativity of the generations before us. The last thing we want to do is dishonor that legacy.

Change is hard. But in our search for a new normal, we have no choice but to change. And we need more than mere triage. We need new ways of doing ministry that lead to long-term, sustainable health.

Our team has been wrestling with tough questions about youth ministry for over a decade and a half. Sticky Faith was the early fruit of that work. Through a series of books, resources, and training, we helped leaders shift their ministries toward developing lifelong faith in order to reverse the trend of youth group graduates walking away from God and the church. We were joined early on by our colleagues Chap Clark and Cheryl Crawford—both practitioner-scholars who wisely called for leaders to face this truth head-on. Chap has returned to serving in pastoral ministry, while Cheryl's life and work were tragically ended by cancer in late 2019. In their honor, Sticky Faith Innovation marks a new chapter in the search for better answers and new ministry imaginations.

We'll be up front here: we can't predict the future. We did not anticipate the state of today's world five years ago at the start of this project. But by God's gracious direction, we prepared for it. Now we couldn't be more excited to share that work with you.

We're especially grateful to have traveled this road with Steve, Caleb, and our talented FYI team. You have in your hands the distillation of thousands of hours of conversations, hundreds of pages of notes, and a mountain of feedback from youth leaders and teenagers; not to mention a legion of embarrassing failures and exciting breakthroughs.

We're proud of this project because it represents the fruit of a journey that started with some faithful, scary steps toward an unknown destination.

And maybe you feel like you are in a similar spot—knowing you need to step out, but hesitant about the first few paces. We believe in the innovation journey. And we believe in you.

Let's get started together.

With you and for you,

Kara Powell

Kara Powell
Executive Director, Fuller Youth Institute

Brad Griffin

Brad M. Griffin
Senior Director of Content, Fuller Youth Institute

CHAPTER ONE

Sticky Faith and Innovation: Meeting Teenagers Where They Need You Most

It was the worst youth ministry mission trip ever. My (Steve's) enthusiasm that convinced our youth group to engage in a service project on the East Coast could not overcome the impact of my poor planning or the current mood of our discouraged teenagers. One of our vehicles broke down. I misjudged how long it would take to make the cross-country trek. My attempts to tell our group that we were "almost there" were increasingly met with eye rolls. I even got a speeding ticket. The police officer who pulled me over gave me a warning and told me, "You're a terrible example!"

When we finally arrived at the worksite (late and exhausted), we were told our team would split up and not be working together. All the teambuilding we prepared for and the vision I painted of us serving together were dashed with the site director's singular instruction. I remember sitting in the parking lot with our dejected group, most of whom were doing their best to pretend they were not mad at me.

Then some of the students began to speak. They reminded each other that this trip was not about them but for the people they came to serve. They spoke to each other about how God is faithful and might faithfully be trying to teach us something. One of them prayed. They rallied. I followed. To this day, some of these students still say it was the best trip they have ever been on.

We got lucky. My planning was poor, but something still happened during that unpredictable mission experience that disrupted the security of friends, control, and predictability.

Those familiar props evaporated and my teenagers had to rely on something more certain—God. My terrible youth pastoring aside, something about that encounter did ring true: life is filled with surprises and unplanned moments. We experience these instabilities in small and large doses. Life's instabilities can detour our direction, mess with our emotions, disrupt our relationships, and force us to reflect on what really matters. In fact, life's instabilities feel more like everyday occurrences than the rare, stable moments!

Ironically, while youth leaders know that teenagers' lives are packed with instability, most youth ministry programming tries to reach them when their lives are stable. Ministry success gets equated with stability. As a result, youth leaders report success by how many students show up at an event, remark that no one got hurt on the mission trip, and celebrate that students are behaving or "getting it, praise the Lord." The more teenagers that fit into their stable youth ministry programs, the more successful youth leaders are deemed.

Some youth leaders—the brave ones—will admit their ministry failures. They want to see their teenagers' faith stick, but can't seem to get beyond the challenges of inconsistent attendance, disruptive behavior, ever-present sports schedules, and unpredictable friend and family drama. It's natural to get anxious, fearing that if they can't manage "successful," stable youth ministries, they may not have a job by year-end.

When youth ministry "success" rests on teenage stability, youth leaders will try to program toward it. Yet teenagers are perpetually navigating *instability*. The gap between teenagers' needs and youth ministry solutions could not be more pronounced. It's time to acknowledge and close this gap.

Keeping up with today's teenagers

Teenagers' lives change and demand new understanding.

It can be tough to keep up.

A decade ago, in an attempt to help youth leaders keep up, Kara Powell, Chap Clark, Brad Griffin, and Cheryl Crawford researched and wrote the groundbreaking Sticky Faith series of books and trainings. These resources continue to animate youth leaders' vision for discipling young people to know and walk with Jesus in their everyday lives. At the Fuller Youth Institute (FYI), our team consistently hears stories of how Sticky Faith principles are forming more robust faith in young people.

This book, *Sticky Faith Innovation*, builds on FYI's original research, expanding ways youth leaders can support the faith journeys of today's—and tomorrow's—teenagers. This is important because youth leaders confess to us that they feel unsure about whether all the energy they pour into their youth ministries is actually developing lasting—or "sticky"—faith in the students they serve.

Teenagers' changing lives need a faith that grows with them.

And they need you.

In new ways.

Through changing circumstances.

To accompany them as their lives grow and their faith sticks.

Sticky Faith Innovation leverages the best of your ministry and encourages you to step into the gaps where your teenagers need you most. It is designed to inspire and lead you to channel your compassion, creativity, and courage toward the pressing needs of your young people.

We believe you want to go there.

After all, that's what youth ministry is all about. But sometimes it takes some fresh perspectives to get there, so let us explain.

New challenges require new ministry approaches

Youth ministry is at a crucial point where improving tried-and-true methods will not get us to the places where young people need the most spiritual support. The call for new approaches is getting louder and more consistent. More youth leaders are admitting that it's harder to keep up with current ministry challenges. Some of you have expressed that you feel stuck and are searching for more effective ways to care for your teenagers. The changing landscape of teenage lives and experiences are forcing all youth leaders to think differently. For example:

How do we create welcoming spaces for teenagers who gather online as much as they do in person?

What kind of partnership do parents, stepparents, guardians, and grandparents need or want?

Is gathering as a youth group creating more stress in our teenagers' already packed schedules? What if we are part of the problem?

How do we do youth ministry in a way that responds to the diversity of our neighborhoods and the diverse needs of our teenagers?

These questions are necessary, but can also feel intimidating because they ask something different from us and our youth ministry work. The goal of this book is to inspire and equip you, the youth leader, to develop tailor-made, fresh ministry approaches that can support your young people's growing faith as they navigate life's changes, challenges, and instabilities.

Searching for identity, belonging, and purpose through instability

You may have heard the phrase, "trying to build the plane while flying it." Teenagers are, quite dramatically, trying to build their lives while living them. Their pilgrimage from childhood toward adulthood requires them to discover and develop their identity, belonging, and purpose, continually asking the questions of *Who am I? Where do I fit?* and *What difference can I make?* For a quick reference and definitions of identity, belonging, and purpose, see the chart on page 23.

> *You may have heard the phrase, "trying to build the plane while flying it." Teenagers are, quite dramatically, trying to build their lives while living them.*

These questions of identity, belonging, and purpose are human questions that people ask and seek to answer throughout their lives. While adults often ask these questions during seasons of major instability (such as moving, having or losing a child, getting married or divorced, and starting or losing a job), teenagers ask these questions every time they face instabilities of any size. In other words—all the time!

Teenagers' instability isn't all bad. Feeling unstable comes with the steps they take toward growing up. For example, they must make many choices, like whether to play on a team, join a drama group, volunteer their time, care for a younger sibling, share their testimony for the first time, stand up for a friend, embrace their racial or ethnic identity, or apply for college or a job. These are all positive growth steps as they learn more about themselves and develop their personal agency and faith. Yet even these healthy choices move them closer toward a more complex, unstable world where they need adult support and accompaniment.

Other elements of teenage instability are thrust upon them by external social forces. For example, they experience more depression and anxiety as they shoulder the pressure to maintain good grades, perfect their image, or try to fit in.[1] Their learning occurs under the grip of discrimination, violence, underfunded schools, or family struggle.[2] Digital technology is often a positive space for connection but is also an arena for comparison, bullying, and shame.[3] These examples and others reveal the broader forces impacting young people who are recipients of social, racial, and economic disparities, injustices, and pressures that exist in our country, which have strong influence on their search for identity, belonging, and purpose. Growing up means that young people will make mistakes and experience new anxieties, but often instability reveals the effects of a demanding system that expects too much while providing too little support.

Whether teenagers are taking healthy steps or facing challenging circumstances, instability surrounds them as they navigate a world of increasing complexity. They need renewed adult support and accompaniment as they search for their true identity, belonging, and purpose.

What teenagers are searching for:

	IDENTITY	BELONGING	PURPOSE
KEY QUESTION	Who am I?	Where do I fit?	What difference can I make?
DESCRIPTION	Young people's view of themselves	Young people's connections to others	Young people's contributions to the world

Teenagers search for *identity* by asking the question, "Who am I?"

To put it simply, identity is young people's view of themselves. Many aspects influence a person's identity, such as beliefs, relationships, family, friendships, religion, ethnicity, social groups, politics, and achievements. Identity is not one-size-fits-all. When you really listen to young people, you begin to uncover and understand the many competing influences they contend with and how their decisions and struggles relate to their search for identity.

Teenagers search for *belonging* by asking the question, "Where do I fit?"

We define belonging as young people's connections to others. People sense they belong when they feel connected to and can trust a community in which they can exert influence, have needs met, and mutually share an emotional connection with others. When you really listen to young people, you can begin to see how these different elements of belonging relate to young people's friendship groups, family dynamics, and their connection to, or disconnection from, church.

*Teenagers search for **purpose** by asking the question, "What difference can I make?"*

Purpose refers to young people's contributions to the world. While we are all called by God to love God and love others, teenagers also desire to discover their unique purpose. Young people with purpose show commitment to what they value, and are able to pursue a goal, find meaning in their efforts, and believe they are making a difference. Understanding these dimensions of purpose can empower you to explore young people's lives, whether they seem to have attained a purpose and whether that purpose aligns with God's story or some other story (like individualism, the American Dream, or the pursuit of pleasure) to help them make meaning of their lives.[4]

Identity, belonging, and purpose

Quests for identity, belonging, and purpose overlap and influence one another. How young people see themselves influences their sense of belonging and purpose. Where young people feel connected influences their view of themselves and whether they believe their lives matter. Their sense of purpose shapes who they are and to whom they feel connected. Talk about instability!

FYI orients a lot of our work around the big questions of identity, belonging, and purpose. For a deep dive into how today's teenagers are exploring these questions and how you and your team can help, check out Kara Powell and Brad Griffin's book *3 Big Questions that Change Every Teenager: Making the Most of Your Conversations and Connections.* Find out more about this and other resources at fulleryouthinstitute.org.

Living faithfully through instability

If we start with the understanding that teenagers are living most of their lives in instability, we can begin imagining what it means to reorient our youth ministries toward their quests for identity, belonging, and purpose—based on *their* realities, not ours.

Shifting our ministry focus toward young people's spaces of instability raises two crucial issues that youth leaders cannot avoid. First, the only way to address instability is to work through it. You cannot avoid it. Second, no teenager graduating from high school can take their youth ministry with them, so you need a formation plan that is portable. Both of these elements are related in that they share a common center—spiritual formation, or discipleship.

In order for faith to form, stick, and grow, teenagers need youth ministries that help them live faithfully in their instability. In fact, the spaces of instability are often the places where teenagers are searching the hardest, as well as most sensitive to God's presence and in greatest need of spiritual support. In the following chapters, we'll call this instability the *gap* where young people need the support of their faith communities and where youth leaders must focus their innovative energies.

For now, remember that we must find and innovate new ways to resource our teenagers so they can develop spiritual habits that inspire their growth and equip them to live faithfully on the move. Deeper formation can happen when we accompany young people through their lived instabilities where plans change, questions surface, challenges arise, disappointments hurt, and faith grows. We can come up with new approaches to ministry that meet teenagers where they need us most. To get there, we need *innovation*.

Innovation with and for youth leaders just like you

We're going to level with you.

We know you may be suspicious of youth ministry books. Oftentimes, new resources with state-of-the-art ideas offer unrealistic expectations from the experts. While leaders like you are gracious, it's easy to get discouraged over one more resource that tells you what you're doing wrong and what you should do instead. We hope you'll find that Sticky Faith Innovation feels different because we approached our research and this book differently.

We partnered closely with other youth leaders like you at every step of the research project that has ultimately led to this book. With the generous funding of Lilly Endowment Inc. and Sacred Harvest Foundation, we launched a 4-year-long research project called Youth Ministry Innovations, which we refer to as our "Sticky Faith Innovation research project." Our research design invited youth leaders to help us develop an effective innovation model that works for leaders to develop fresh ministry approaches. Our work together made the research successful as youth leaders tested the model, collected data, and came up with innovative, new approaches in their ministries.

This project only succeeded because more than 100 youth leaders from more than 50 churches across the country risked learning and creating together with us. From 50-person churches with four teenagers to 4,500-person churches with hundreds of students (and everywhere in between), representing over 13 different denominations, these leaders showed us that innovation was possible and transformative.[5] *Sticky Faith Innovation* is the fruit of our shared journey. Throughout the rest of this book, you'll hear many of their stories that we hope will inspire your own.

Innovation and practical theology

While many industries use the term "innovation," we intend to apply it uniquely to ministry contexts by rooting it in Christian practical theology. Practical theology is a process Christian leaders use to ensure that their ministries are both relevant to the people under their care and faithful to the gospel.

Generally, the process has four elements:

1. Naming the problem
   (What's happening?)

2. Analyzing the situation
   (What do Scripture and research say about it?)

3. Discerning next steps
   (What shall we do in light of our context and culture?)

4. Activating those steps
   (How shall we implement the steps we must take?)[6]

In many ways, Sticky Faith Innovation mirrors this pattern, integrating tools from design thinking, to guide youth leaders as they respond faithfully and effectively to the young people they care about.[7]

How to get the most out of this book

Each reader comes with different backgrounds, perspectives, needs, and hopes. We know that you are experts in your contexts, so we have designed this book to be a resource that you can work through by yourself, read with other youth leaders, use to train your teams, and keep coming back to. With that in mind, the following scenarios may capture where you are starting in your innovation process:

I need to come up with some new ideas right now

A large part of innovation is simply trying new ideas. Often leaders need some first steps to get them going. At the end of Chapters 2 through 8, you will find how-to exercises that provide specific instructions on how to implement the Sticky Faith Innovation process. We hope these practical sections help you make your first innovation moves to develop new ideas.

I need to see the big picture before I give this a try

Perhaps you're a conceptual thinker who wants to understand the method behind the madness. Each chapter draws from our research, backed by a conceptual framework, quantitative data collection, and qualitative feedback. Every practical step is rooted in our tested framework so you can not only do the exercises but also learn the process. You may want to read each of the major chapters in their entirety, skimming the how-to exercises, until you understand the big picture. Then, go back more slowly through the how-to exercises for practical ways to implement each essential step.

I need to know this innovation process actually works

We were thrilled to see what youth leaders and their teams developed. Churches just like yours worked through this process and many of them experienced exciting results. For those of you who need to see some examples of what real churches created, jump over to Chapter 9. We hope your ministry will add to these inspiring stories!

I need to train my team toward a new way of thinking

We find that leaders who include their teams in this process experience greater innovation, team-building, and overall better results. If you are thinking about how to invest in your team, we encourage you to get a copy of this book for each of the team members you want to journey with you. The main chapters will deepen everyone's understanding of the process, and the how-to exercises at the end of each chapter will help you implement the process together. Sometimes the hardest part of training your team is having to develop materials to implement a book's great ideas. We've done that work for you!

I want to be an innovative leader who inspires my faith community

We hear you. We've been there. For some youth leaders, the highlight of this book will be the new ideas and methods that have the potential to move your ministry closer to young people and empower you to make needed changes both now and in the future. We've worked with many leaders who feared their youth ministries (and churches) were too stuck in their ways. Sticky Faith Innovation helped them get unstuck. We encourage you to invest in the entire innovation process to build the confidence you need to take your ministry where it needs to go. The magic happens when you walk step by step through each move, which will ultimately lead you to develop more responsive ministries that support young people where they need the church the most.

Sticky Faith Innovation has the promise to be transformational for you too, growing you into an innovative leader—someone who is adept, discerning, and courageous in how you serve teenagers in our ever-changing world. There's more here than trying to "change teenagers." This process holds the potential to change you, which may be the exciting and terrifying invitation you've been searching for.

REFLECT

1. Think about your life. What memories do you have of experiencing instability as a teenager? How did these hopeful or challenging moments shape your identity, belonging, and purpose? What kind of support did you have (or wish you had)?

REFLECT

2. Take a minute to reflect on some of the teenagers in your ministry. What do their instabilities look like? Jot down the positive and negative elements that create the instability they are navigating throughout middle and high school.

REFLECT

3. Think about your youth ministry. Where do you see it being responsive and supportive to teenagers' lives of instability? Where might your students need the church the most but your ministry is currently offering the least support?

CHAPTER TWO

Sticky Faith Innovation's Three Moves: Compassion, Creativity, and Courage

"I don't know what I'm doing,"

said most youth leaders.

Out loud.

To no one.

In youth ministry, it can be hard to admit when we feel like we don't exactly know what we're doing or where we're going. It probably didn't seem that way when you started; or at least you didn't notice. Enthusiasm and instincts can fuel our ministry drive for a while. Confidence can run high at first—especially after a few initial successes—but as the months drag on, the way forward often gets blurred.

In fact, it's likely that the more you've gotten to know your teenagers, the more you're realizing that a great talk, an awesome retreat, or your contagious adrenaline can't reach some of the deep and complex circumstances they're navigating. Their lives of instability and your solutions seem light years apart. And the compassion, creativity, and courage that once led you into youth ministry can suddenly evaporate without warning.

In youth ministry, it can be easy to fall into a "fake it 'til you make it" existence. We've all hit the youth ministry wall (or if you're new to ministry, you eventually will) where our next moves seem unclear and even our own calling feels uncertain.

It's hard to admit this out loud, though. Admitting when we're stuck runs the risk of looking incompetent or, even worse, irrelevant.

It's even natural to panic as you try to recover. Perhaps you're tempted to copy and paste from other ministries, hoping the tried-and-true methods of others can at least keep the attendance numbers up. Or you make big promises that are impossible to keep. Or you lay low, playing it safe, just trying to stay off of parents' and church leaders' radars by making as few waves as possible.

Now youth ministry feels like survival.

And we all want more than that.

You want more.

You long for a way forward.

For teenagers. And for you.

You're not weird if you feel this way. The world is changing at a rate that is leaving not only youth leaders but leaders from nearly every sector of society (including your boss) uncertain about the future of their industries and their place in them. If you are feeling lost or stuck, it's not because you're incompetent. It is more likely you are in this liminal space (instability!) where old habits cannot keep up with your current challenges. Brave leaders admit when they are stuck and start looking for new ways forward.

That's you.

In fact, we've written this book with a pretty important assumption in mind—you already have the compassion, creativity, and courage you need to serve your teenagers in your youth ministry. You just need to call them out of hiding and channel them in the right direction.

The three moves of Sticky Faith Innovation

Sticky Faith Innovation guides you through three crucial moves—compassion, creativity, and courage. This innovation process is designed to help you and your youth ministry team deepen your compassion as you learn more about your teenagers today, unleash your creativity for new solutions, and leverage your courage to take that next faithful step your ministry needs and your young people want.

Here's a quick overview of where we're heading.

COMPASSION

Innovation starts with focusing on people, not programs. It is crucial for youth leaders to invest time to understand their teenagers today in order to support them where they need adults most. Sticky Faith Innovation's move toward more *compassion* invites youth leaders to take two crucial steps: *empathizing with today's teenagers* and *interpreting the messages that shape teenagers' lives.*

Empathizing puts young people first in your ministry—their perspectives, their feelings, their needs.[8] This initial step is the foundation of innovation. It has the potential to radically shift your assumptions about even the young people you think you know well so you can reorient your youth ministry toward young people's most pressing needs.

Interpreting the messages you are hearing allows you to understand teenagers' current answers to their questions of identity, belonging, and purpose and discern the Jesus-centered answers that can set them free. Chapters 3 and 4 walk through how to start innovation through compassion.

CREATIVITY

Sticky Faith Innovation's next move toward creativity prepares you and your team to learn new ways to solve problems and create solutions that are faithfully responsive to where your teenagers need you now. The *creativity* move requires two key steps: *expanding your ministry imagination* and narrowing *toward your best idea* to support teenagers' lasting faith.

Expanding your creative process helps you imagine new ideas and collaborate with your team, taking you beyond your typical brainstorming session. This step can help you deliver better ministry solutions and foster deeper trust. It's the kind of creativity that's contagious and unifying.

Narrowing helps you and your team choose a viable new ministry approach. This step requires more than voting for the most popular idea. Rather, it invites your team into a discernment process to choose your best idea at the point of your teenagers' greatest need. Great narrowing turns your creative ideas into priorities and sets you up to implement them. Chapters 5 and 6 explain how to fuel innovation through creativity.

COURAGE

Sticky Faith Innovation's final move leverages your courage by guiding you and your team to test your innovative idea before you launch it, and then go for it! Courageous initiatives start small, are tested with feedback, invite participation, gather support, and prepare for maximum success. The *courage* move requires two essential steps: *experimenting with your best idea* and *launching your new approach*.

Experimenting helps you gain initial input from teenagers and adults so you can improve your new approach before you launch. *Launching* prepares your team and educates your congregation so you'll be ready to make your innovative idea a reality and support your teenagers' lasting faith. Chapters 7 and 8 show how innovation succeeds through courage.

Combined, these three essential moves and the six steps that support them make up the Sticky Faith Innovation process. Each move's two steps build on each other so you can strategically and faithfully move your ministry in the direction teenagers need you most.

The Sticky Faith Innovation Process

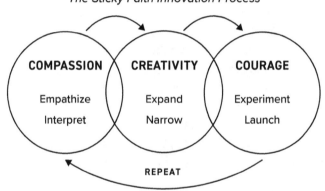

Sticky Faith Innovation—together

Sticky Faith Innovation's goal of supporting teenagers where they need us most relies on the compassion, creativity, and courage of our faith communities. It takes shared wisdom, teamwork, and resources to truly make a difference in our ministries with teenagers.

Building your team

Sticky Faith Innovation calls youth leaders out of isolation into a shared journey of compassion, creativity, and courage. In other words, you can't (nor would you want to) complete this process on your own.

Every step invites you to collaborate, learn together, and grow in mutual support. Each move promises not only to help you develop new ideas, but also to empower you to develop your volunteers and team. Discipleship can happen here. This process has the potential to move not just you, but your leaders, your whole ministry, and your entire church closer to the teenagers you love and serve. In the how-to exercises at the end of this chapter, we'll provide you with a guide to building two crucial Sticky Faith Innovation teams.

Broadening your vision

It's natural for leaders and teams to lose their way at times and to feel isolated. It happens to all of us. Sticky Faith Innovation acknowledges this challenge and provides a way for you to not only get on track but to join the hundreds of leaders we worked with and the other thousands who quietly admit they are looking for new ways forward. Chapter 9 offers snapshots of youth ministries just like yours whose innovations can inspire your imagination. Finally, Chapter 10 shows you how the Sticky Faith Innovation process can both transform your youth ministry posture and shape your congregational culture.

We believe Sticky Faith Innovation has the potential to reshape every youth leader's conversations about their teenagers, ministries, aspirations, and even themselves. Imagine having conversations with other youth leaders who ask, "What's something new you're learning about your teenagers?" "What creative idea have you thought of lately?" and "What risks are you taking for your young people?" These are the conversations that every youth leader longs for.

And even more, Sticky Faith Innovation has the potential to move your ministry closer to your teenagers' lives of instability to help them find and grow a faith that lasts.

REFLECT

1. Think about your ministry. Where do you feel most encouraged? Where do you need new tools to move forward? Take a minute to jot down your reflections. Then ask God how these areas might be signs of opportunity in your ministry and calling.

REFLECT

2. Any step into new territory comes with both
   potential and risks. In what ways do you think
   innovating in your ministry will bring about new
   opportunities and challenges?

REFLECT

3. Remember, even if you feel like you don't know the future of your ministry, you don't have to discern your next ministry step alone. As you begin the Sticky Faith Innovation journey, who comes to mind as someone you could ask to join you?

HOW-TO EXERCISES FOR BUILDING INNOVATION TEAMS

Through our research, we discovered that leaders who built diverse, collaborative teams generated more creative, responsive, and faithful ministry approaches. The variety of perspectives led to more well-thought-out ministry experiments, the increased participation led to unified buy-in, and team members learned more about their strengths, weaknesses, and blind spots.

To start you off on the right foot, these how-to exercises will help you identify leaders for two important teams:

Team 1 is your *innovation team*. This team will learn and engage the Sticky Faith Innovation process with you.

Team 2 is your *discernment team*. This team can help you look at ideas from different points of view as you develop new ministry approaches for your faith community.

I found that many of our team's best ideas didn't actually come from me. It was amazing to see our volunteer leaders shaping the way forward in our ministries in a way I could never have on my own.
—Colton, youth leader

Team 1: Your innovation team

Your innovation team includes those who will navigate the whole innovation process with you. Together, you will:

- tap into your compassion to empathize with young people's everyday instabilities and experiences and interpret what you hear,

- creatively expand your ministry imaginations and narrow to the very best of your ideas,

- and harness your courage to experiment with your best idea and launch your new ministry approach.

As you build this innovation team of (ideally) 3–6 people, consider individuals who come from a variety of backgrounds, including age, ethnicity, race, gender, education, profession, and socioeconomic status. When building your innovation team, you might consider including one person (or more) per prompt below. Go ahead and start jotting down names that come to mind in the spaces provided. Ask God to inspire your thinking.

1. Which adults in your community seem to really understand teenagers well? This might be a parent, someone involved in pastoral care, a teacher, a trained therapist from your congregation, or anyone who listens well to young people. While innovation begins with compassion and empathy, it's essential to maintain an empathetic posture throughout the entire process.

2. Who exhibits creativity and is always thinking of new ways of doing things? This might be an artist from the congregation, someone you often hear saying things like "What if ...?", or a newer person to the congregation who offers a fresh perspective.

3. Who can help your team stay organized and keep moving forward? Perhaps this is a project manager from your church, a ministry assistant, or you.

4. Which teenagers exhibit maturity and leadership potential in your ministry?

5. Of the names you recorded above, make an ordered list of who you would like to invite first to join the innovation team:

1.

2.

3.

4.

5.

6.

7.

8.

9.

10.

With this team, you won't be alone as you collaboratively discern fresh approaches to ministry with teenagers.

Sample innovation team member expectations:

1. Participate in 2–3 innovation team meetings per month.

2. Commit to participation in 3–12 months of innovative work (depending on how much concentrated time and focus you'll be dedicating to the Sticky Faith Innovation process).

3. Listen to teenagers, take notes, participate in brainstorming, and collaboratively design and implement a new ministry approach.

Team 2: Your discernment team

While the innovation team is in the trenches of innovation, the discernment team offers outside perspective and insight into any potential new ministry approach's impact on other areas of the church. Discernment team members often become advocates for innovative approaches that impact not only the youth ministry but the entire church. You need this team to:

- pray for you

- support you

- help you and the innovation team see what you can't on your own

Consider including individuals who come from a variety of backgrounds, including age, ethnicity, race, gender, education, and socioeconomic status.

When building your discernment team, you might consider including one person (or more) per prompt below. Go ahead and start jotting down names that come to mind in the spaces provided.

1. Which church leaders (those with the authority to sign off on ministry decisions) could support your innovation team and help you navigate church power dynamics and decision-making procedures?

2. Which parents and volunteer leaders, who are personally invested in your ministry with young people, might provide you valuable insight that your innovation team may not have?

3. Which other teenagers might give your innovation team additional insight into how your new approach might be received by other students? (You may want to consider those who exhibit maturity and leadership potential, but who don't have enough time to commit to the innovation team.)

Sample discernment team member expectations

1. Read monthly updates from the innovation team.

2. Participate in an innovation team meeting every other month.

3. Offer prayer, insight, and guidance for the innovation team.

In our first Sticky Faith Innovation research cohort, we didn't ask each church to develop a discernment team. That was a mistake. A very wise youth leader took our FYI team aside and said, "I wish there was a step or two in the process that included communal discernment. We need other perspectives outside of our own."[9] This leader's feedback helped us realize that innovation teams aren't enough. Faithful innovation requires the wisdom of the whole community! Leaders from later cohorts expressed so much gratitude for the added wisdom, perspective, and prayers of those who formed their discernment teams. We trust you will as well.

After you build these two teams, you're ready to start the first move of Sticky Faith Innovation—
compassion.

If you would like a seasoned guide or coach on this innovation journey, check out stickyfaithinnovation.com/**training** for opportunities to gain additional support from the FYI team. We'd love to walk with you every step of the way.

Now

You're not alone.

You are developing a team of people who will share the Sticky Faith Innovation process with you.

You're ready to start the next step!

COMPASSION

We start with people, not programs,
Where empathizing brings us closer to their stories,
And interpreting gives us the fluency for understanding, hope, and good news.

"Rejoice with those who rejoice; mourn with those who mourn."

—Romans 12:15

CHAPTER THREE

Empathize with Today's Teenagers: Prioritizing People over Programs

The Sticky Faith Innovation Process

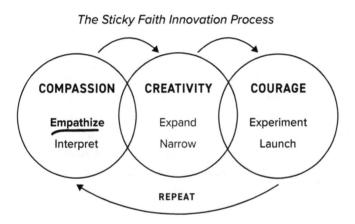

Stopping to listen to the teenagers in our church and community made me realize how much I had assumed teenagers today are just like the millennials I'm used to working with. Empathizing helped me learn new things about who young people are today.

—Christian, youth leader

Over coffee, Trevor, a youth leader, confessed his struggle to connect with teenagers younger than him.

"You know, these middle schoolers are so different from me. I can barely keep up with their new technology, cultural references, or everyday challenges. Sometimes I find it hard to understand where they are coming from compared to when I was in middle school. They're so different!"

Trevor was 17 years old.

Whenever we encounter young people, we remember that conversation. Barely three years older than the middle schoolers themselves, Trevor was self-aware enough to recognize how different his middle school experiences were from the young guys he was mentoring. His perspective raises an essential truth we try hard not to forget—that being a teenager once does not mean we understand teenagers today.

Just because we were teenagers once does not mean we understand teenagers' experiences today.

This is a good reminder for all adults and even more essential for youth leaders. You see, sometimes we youth leaders—those who work closely with teenagers—can make more assumptions and pay less attention. Youth leaders in our Sticky Faith Innovation research remarked how important it was that they recommit to paying attention to the unique teenagers they serve. In fact, the listening exercise we assigned to each church (and the one we'll guide you through in the how-to section at the end of the chapter) had a profound impact on youth leaders. For example, one youth leader, Christian, confessed, "Stopping to listen to the teenagers in our church and community made me realize how much I had assumed teenagers today are just like the millennials I'm used to working with. Empathizing helped me learn new things about who young people are today."

Our notions of young people must continually be tested and adjusted to track with teenagers' rapidly changing lives. We may find ourselves surprised, like Trevor, or challenged, like Christian. Yet these are hopeful signs that we are seeking to know our teenagers today rather than relying on yesterday's assumptions.

Youth ministry's most powerful force (you) and biggest barrier (again, you)

Perhaps you can relate to Trevor's and Christian's reflections. In theory, it makes sense. The older we get, the further we find ourselves from current teenage experiences. Youth leaders who fail to see the truth of these honest insights often embarrass themselves when they try to relate to teenagers by reliving high school or being "hip with the kids." More subtly, even though most leaders acknowledge generational differences, we still believe they can connect with teenagers. And we find that our ability to connect with teenagers reveals the gift we have and the barriers we face.

The gift youth leaders have

Perhaps you are a youth leader today because, as a young person, you were impacted positively by an adult. You remember navigating the mysterious teenage years and can still feel the residual emotions associated with loneliness, trying to fit in, discovering your talents, or getting cut from the team. You remember the people who were there for you—a parent, grandparent, teacher, youth pastor, or mentor—and you want to pay that support forward. Maybe this is even a moment to pause and thank God for those essential people in your life. Perhaps it's even worth it to put this book down and take a minute to text or call them to thank them.

Youth leaders are truly unique because you are a rare breed of adults who actually feel comfortable being around a group of teenagers. Ask the typical adult to walk into a room full of adolescents and just watch their body language! Youth leaders instinctively seek out young people because you find them amazing, interesting people. At high school sports events, you leave the safety of the parents' section to talk with students. At family reunions, you gravitate toward teenagers. At FYI, we remind the youth leaders we train that there is one skill we never have to teach them—to care about young people. When it comes to love and compassion for teenagers, you are already way ahead of the curve.

The barriers youth leaders must navigate

Yet you may be sensing that some of your youth ministry superpowers are waning and you're not exactly sure why. While this section may feel a bit more technical, it may also give some insights to what you're experiencing. Awareness of *intragenerational speed* and *closeness bias* can make us more attuned to the work we need to do to remain connected with today's teenagers.

Intragenerational speed. Understanding young people is harder today not only because of obvious intergenerational differences, but also because of the speed at which society is changing. The dramatic pace of technological, scientific, medical, economic, and sociological shifts is creating more differences *within* traditional generational cohorts than ever before. For example, it's common to witness two siblings gravitating towards two different social media platforms to connect with their friends even though they're only a few years apart. Or consider that teenagers now have a choice to attend school online (even pre-pandemic), which was unthinkable only a few years ago.

The rate of change within a traditional generational period is speeding up. Now, four or five "generations" exist within a 20-year generational cycle.[10] This phenomenon is known as *intragenerational.*[11] When we talk about young people, we must remember that they are young "peoples" whose experiences, habits, beliefs, worldviews, and relationships shift and change with every incoming freshman class.

When Trevor said his middle schoolers are so different, he was right. We cannot assume common experiences between or even within generations anymore. We must pay even closer attention.

Closeness bias. This second barrier warns us that the closer we are to others relationally, the less connected we can become. Some research shows that close relationships breed familiarity, and familiarity causes people to make assumptions about their friends, partners, and kids.[12] When this happens, relationships can disintegrate because people stop seeking to learn about each other. For youth leaders, this is a crucial warning. If we claim to professionally "know young people," we risk letting our expertise, dated assumptions, or familiarity blind us to seeing, hearing, and understanding teenagers today. More than ever, youth ministry work requires listening closely so that we can accurately know young people and serve them well.

Make no mistake, youth leaders are uniquely gifted for and passionate about working with teenagers. But based on the speed of life (intragenerational speed) and youth leaders' familiarity with young people (closeness bias), we must keep listening to the worlds, experiences, and needs

We are a young church plant that prides ourselves on thinking creatively, yet ... we, too, have a hard time diverging from what we've "always done."

—Cassandra, youth leader

of teenagers today. Without warning, misinformed assumptions can lead us to ask the wrong questions, offer the wrong help, and miss the young people we care about altogether.

Sticky Faith Innovation starts with people, not programs

We believe any attempt to support teenagers must begin with empathy—which may seem obvious, but has not always been the case because of two powerful forces. First, we youth leaders can confuse our dedication to young people with empathy for young people. We all run the risk of missing the needs of *today's* teenagers.

Second, we youth leaders can be a little too proud of our ministry programming. Our traditions, planning, and creativity can lull us into thinking our work is good and that teenagers just need to see how great it is. One youth leader, Cassandra, admitted, "We are a young church plant that prides ourselves on thinking creatively, yet it's amazing how quickly we've created our own types of traditions and expectations. We, too, have a hard time diverging from what we've 'always done.'"

When leaders see a drop in attendance, they might think they have a "marketing problem" and spend even more time promoting their programs rather than listening to their people. This is a mistake.

Starting with our people, not our programs, requires empathy.

Empathy's challenge: stepping closer (for real)

Any youth leader worth their role knows that empathy is important—and we certainly know that you, youth leader, are not *un*-empathetic. Remember, however, that empathy is more than a feeling or aspiration. It is actually a skill that helps us tune in to the people we serve.

Youth leaders are known to express frustration that sports, school, parents, secularism, or the internet have somehow made young people "less committed" to church or youth group. While these factors may have some impact, youth leaders might need to critique themselves first. A better approach is for leaders to reimagine what young people need, rather than judging them for not attending a program. If youth ministry digs its heels in, demanding allegiance to its old forms, it forces young people to make a false choice between church and (fill in the blank with your favorite villain). When we do this, we set up young people to lose every time.

We also know from research that even if young people show up to ministry programming, they may not really reveal their true selves. More likely, they will perform for adults, telling them what they want to hear in order to keep the peace. Therefore, even when teenagers choose to show up, it does not automatically mean they are engaging youth leaders with their authentic selves.[13]

Youth ministry programming runs the risk of pretending to connect with young people when it is actually creating more distance between leaders and teenagers. It can be tempting to do things for young people without really having to engage their real lives. Inviting teenagers to attend youth group is easier and more efficient than engaging each of them in conversation. Yet if we're not careful, programs will distance us from the very teenage lives we care about.[14]

Empathy's power to change us

Empathy is the way we attempt to understand others, feel their emotions, and seek to see the world through their perspectives. It helps us pause before we move too quickly to critique teenagers' actions or rush to give them advice. Empathy not only helps young people; it can transform us.

Empathy is "listening, holding space, withholding judgment, emotionally connecting, and communicating that incredibly healing message of 'You're not alone.'"
—Brené Brown, author and researcher

We acquire abilities to see and even feel teenagers' points of view.

We generate skills to more accurately assess and respond to young people's circumstances.

We are moved to action to support teenagers where they need us most.[15]

Empathizing challenges us to put teenagers, their perspectives, their feelings, and their needs first. It requires that we risk stepping closer to appreciate teenagers' lives and worlds. Researcher Brené Brown puts it simply and powerfully: Empathy is "listening, holding space, withholding judgment, emotionally connecting, and communicating that incredibly healing message of 'You're not alone.'"[16]

This is a deeply Christian move.

Empathy's Christian vision

Our Christian motivation for empathy is rooted in the ministry of Jesus. Paul's compelling hymn in Philippians 2 emphatically speaks to the moves Jesus made toward humanity. The writer of Hebrews speaks of Jesus as the great high priest and advocate who is able to empathize with our humanity (Hebrews 4:15). The Gospel writers testify to a very human savior who laughs, cries, gets angry, holds children, befriends outcasts, hugs lepers, and travels with disciples (some of whom were likely teenagers!). Jesus' actions must be seen as more than illustrations or ministry examples. His life expressed good news fueled by his perspective-taking empathy. His actions, perhaps even more than his words, compelled many to follow him and others to want to kill him.[17] The gospel has always been and must be more than words. It is always in-person.

Empathy's posture

We miss the point if we look to Jesus and suggest that we should just "do what Jesus did." This idea breaks down quickly because none of us can claim the role of Jesus. What we can offer is Jesus' presence as we disciple and empathize with others. Jesus promises in Matthew 28:20 that he will be with us always as we continue his work on earth. This is more than a sentimental parting remark from someone who is going to miss his friends. This is a promise that, when we seek to empathetically step closer to others, we, too, encounter the living Christ. We experience brushes with the holy.

Empathizing moves us toward holy ground where we encounter each other and are faced with hearing, feeling, and sharing our life stories. Jesus' promised, holy presence may convict us, break our hearts, evoke our insecurities, and overwhelm us with love. Jesus' presence compels us to listen, love, care, and even help. This may be why empathy in ministry is often so difficult. It requires us to follow Jesus into these holy moments. But honestly, it is the *only* way. Ministry at a distance is not ministry at all. Attempting to share the gospel at a distance is rarely good news.

So what might happen in encounters with the holy?

We tie our line to others. We can no longer assume someone else will handle a person's story. Empathy connects us to others and intertwines our stories. "Teenagers" now have names and faces. The gospel becomes more specific and requires our investment, which promises to be both messy and beautiful.

We risk having our worldviews challenged and changed. Empathy compels us to understand others' perspectives. Our own assumptions could be challenged and this might feel disruptive. Empathy will likely change us as much as it helps others.

Our hearts break and we face our limitations. You might believe that empathy is important, but you also might be wondering, "Can I empathize with everyone?" There is a difference between everyone deserving empathy and you doing it all. As a leader, your job will be to train others in the priority of empathy, preparing them for the joy and challenge this will bring. Empathy exposes our limitations while expanding our hearts.

We lead with understanding. Many leaders remark that while empathy is a good practice, they feel they have an obligation to "speak the truth." Remember that seeking to empathize with teenagers is not about agreeing or disagreeing with them, it is about seeking to understand them first.

Empathy's presence *will* challenge us and even change us. When we seek to serve others, we are embarking on an all-in, life-to-life, mutually transforming endeavor that is good news for everyone. Anything less leaves youth ministry retreating to safe programming and distanced relationships. As youth leaders, you invest in young people because you think they truly matter. Empathy inspires us to step toward teenagers, hang in there, and not walk away.

Empathy's starting point

Youth leaders can become more empathetic by recommitting to listen to young people. Practicing empathy empowers us to see teenagers as experts on their own lives and ourselves as interested novices who are willing to learn.

This posture requires a willingness to release control and elevate the voices and stories of teenagers first. What do teenagers care about? What do they fear? Where do they feel freedom, pressure, pain, hope, or confusion? Great listening requires skills like:

Trust. Our role does not earn us the right for a teenager to reveal anything to us. Relationally, teenagers need to know they can trust you, that you will listen generously, and that you will hold their story carefully.

Patience. Programming shouldn't define the conversational timeline—teenagers should. Teenagers will reveal what they choose to, in their time, and in their way. As leaders, we must wait patiently. Any attempt to force a subject hurts more than it helps.

Maturity. We need to be able to handle teenagers' stories. If you feel uncomfortable with the stories your students reveal, seek out a mentor's guidance. Perhaps the story reveals something about your own past and you may need to reach out for counseling. If you are afraid of their story, this says more about you than them.

Responsiveness. We must know how to respond to the stories teenagers share. Joking, silence, anger, or shame will bring more hurt than healing. Teenagers need affirmation, support, love, assurance, and sometimes professional help. Recognize that if you are really open to listening empathetically, your ministry work will increase, not decrease. Yet you'll be doing the right work. As many youth leaders from our research reflected, the extra work is worth it.

Renewed, empathetic listening will require multiple attempts, short conversations, trust-building, and patience to wait until teenagers are ready to reveal the real parts of who they are.

These are the sacred spaces adults cannot force and only young people can freely offer. If teenagers feel like they can truly open up, it is the youth leader's role to listen, seek to understand, and honor the moment. Leaders who attempted this listening posture in our research made some significant discoveries that often changed them. For example, Josiah described his listening experience this way:

As I tried to really listen to one of my students, I realized that maybe I was being too quick to respond with advice or a "truth" and that it was actually holding him back. We've spoken a lot over this week (we normally do) and I've tried harder to understand where he's coming from and what he's struggling with, even when he says something that often seems out of left field.

In particular, he often asks questions about whether he belongs, and talks about his loneliness and feelings of rejection. My immediate response has always been to explain to him that he is welcome in our group and in our community, and we are not excluding him. But this week I've tried to say fewer things to counter him immediately. Instead, I tried to just get him to unpack his thoughts and talk through the feelings he has, and attempt to see things from his perspective. And now I feel I'm starting to understand him better—that no matter how good or bad his current circumstances, his perspective is being colored by his past experiences, and he is struggling to move past fears that have built up and stayed unaddressed for most of his life.

Norene, another youth leader, put it this way: "When you learn to sit back and listen to what they have to say, they become much more transparent, opening up, willing to be seen."

Listening with empathy draws leaders to teenagers' sides where they learn to appreciate and even feel what young people are going through. It humanizes everyone. This is accompaniment.

Empathy's hope

Our task is to accompany teenagers in their spaces of instability that are inspiring, painful, hopeful, challenging, and even gut-wrenching. God calls youth leaders to proclaim good news by first and foremost stepping closer toward teenagers when the world often steps away.

Young people need us to join them in their journeys, not sign them up for ours. Empathy guides the way.

When you learn to sit back and listen to what they have to say, they become much more transparent, opening up, willing to be seen.

—Norene, youth leader

REFLECT

1. How do you typically keep up on the latest trends regarding teenagers? Where do you feel up to date? Where are you feeling out of the loop?

REFLECT

2. How do you specifically keep up with the lives of teenagers in your community? How do you seek to understand them?

REFLECT

3. Read this chapter's description of empathy again on page 62. On a scale from 1 to 5, rate your faith community's empathy with today's teenagers. Where would you rate your own empathy on this scale? Your youth ministry leaders? Parents? Church leadership?

5 Very empathetic

4

3

2

1 Not empathetic at all

REFLECT

4. Empathy is not easy. This chapter explores ways that empathy can be hard on page 58. Which of these challenges have you felt or experienced?

REFLECT

5. Listening can help us be more empathetic.
   Reflect on a time when someone really
   empathized with you. How did you feel?

HOW-TO EXERCISES FOR EMPATHIZING

We've created a listening guide to get you started with empathizing with your teenagers. As you and your innovation team try this exercise, remember that empathy is more than a formula—it's a posture.

This listening exercise begins with a fairly simple premise—we want to frame our thinking by beginning with young people, not our programming. What this means is that before we launch any new programs *for* teenagers in our communities, we invest time *with* them, listening and empathizing with their stories and perspectives.

You and your innovation team likely have a wide range of experiences. Some on your team confidently interact with teenagers all the time. Others may be learning. Use the following instructions to help you and your leaders as you see fit.

This exercise can be an opportunity for you and your innovation team members to recommit to listening to teenagers by reaching out to more of them and inviting them to teach you about their lives.

These how-to exercises will equip you by:

1. Providing you a list of questions to ask your students. You can use this list of questions or adjust them for your context.

2. Explaining how you can capture your notes by summarizing them in order to reflect on the most pressing themes your students share.

Listening preparation checklist

☐ Check with your leadership to clarify whether you need parental permission to meet with teenagers and for any protocols on appropriate ways to meet with them.

☐ Invite and schedule meetings with a wide range of students who vary by age, gender, and background.

☐ Bring what you need to take notes immediately following each conversation.

☐ Schedule a time to meet as an innovation team after each team member has completed their interviews.

☐ Schedule a time to meet with or update your discernment team (after all of your listening and processing is completed as an innovation team).

Listening and conversation tips

- Start each conversation by thanking the teenager for getting together. Remind the young person that your ministry is working to better understand teenagers and that you think he or she could offer a helpful perspective.

- Let the student know there are no wrong answers and that you will only share what you hear with your leadership team, who is also meeting up with students.

- Be aware of your posture. Think of your interview as a conversation—not a Bible quiz or Q&A session with an expert.

- Pay close attention. Save note-taking for when the conversation is finished.

- Be prepared to ask clarifying questions. Don't assume you know what they mean. For example, if a student says, "Yeah, friendships are really hard sometimes." Follow up with, "Tell me more about that. How are they hard? Can you give me an example?"

- Lastly, resist the urge to give advice, a challenge, or explanation for responses teenagers give, even if you disagree or have a different perspective. This isn't meant to be a mentoring session; it's a learning session for you and your innovation team!

 This isn't meant to be a mentoring session; it's a learning session for you and your innovation team!

Listening Questions

Use some of these questions, all of them, or make your own![18]

1. Tell me a little bit about a typical day in your life. What do you do, where do you go, who are you around? That kind of thing.

2. Who would you say are one or two of your closest friends? Why do you like being with them? What do you do together?

3. If I asked a couple of those close friends to describe you, what do you think they'd say?

4. What's it like to be a teenager today? In other words, what's something most adults don't know about people your age, but you think we should know?

5. Can you think of any particularly important moments in your faith that stand out to you? Maybe a time when you really experienced God (or felt God's presence)—what was that like, and why was it meaningful?

6. Do one or two people come to mind who have impacted your life or faith? Tell me a little bit about them and why they've been important to you.

7. What do you love most about our church? Is there a particular story that comes to mind or a specific example?

8. What do you hope or dream for the future of our church? What do you wish was different?

9. Where do you really feel like you belong, no matter what? Who are the people with whom you feel the most yourself?

10. When someone asks you, "What do you want to do with your life?" or "What do you want to be when you grow up?" What kinds of reactions do you have? What do you feel or think about?

11. Can you describe some of the hardest or more challenging parts of your life? What is stressful, hard, or confusing to you? [Follow-up question: How do you deal with that?]

12. How can we as a church be supporting you and other teenagers right now?

13. What's one thing about you that's important to know, that you think I may not have asked about or you didn't get a chance to say?

Comparing notes and discovering themes

Once your innovation team members have interviewed students and recorded their notes, your team will meet back together to share what you heard in your conversations. Remember, when you share your notes with each other, you are NOT interpreting your students' responses. You are only trying to capture and summarize what they shared with you.

1. Once all innovation team members have taken turns sharing their observations, start to find common themes you notice across all your interviews. Try answering the following questions and take notes about your answers. Your work here will set you up to connect these themes to teenagers' identity, belonging, and purpose in the next step.

a. Were there any common themes your students shared?

b. What confirmed what you already knew of teenagers?

c. What surprised you?

2. During the meeting, take some time to pray together for the teenagers you each interviewed. How might God be speaking to you and your church through these teenagers' stories and perspectives?

a. Pray over the emotions your students are holding (fear, anxiety, hope, anger, etc.).

b. Pray over the concerns they raise (friends, family, work, school, neighborhood, future, etc.).

c. Pray over the hopes they have.

d. Pray that God would foster more empathy in your church for young people.

Now

You are listening to teenagers.

You are seeking to understand them from their perspectives.

You are preparing to accompany them as you step closer and put them first.

Great job!

CHAPTER FOUR

Interpret the Messages that Shape Teenagers' Lives:
Finding the Gap between Current and Jesus-Centered Answers

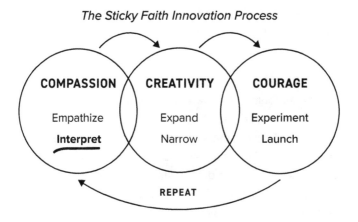

The Sticky Faith Innovation Process

Sticky Faith Innovation transformed the way our adults interacted with students. We interpreted where they were in their spiritual journeys and got to walk alongside them as they worked to discover their ultimate purpose for the kingdom of God.

—Aiysha, youth leader

Sticky Faith Innovation leads with *compassion* because most adults (including us!) can't remember their teenage experiences very well. Any adult who tells you they "loved middle school" or says that high school was "no big deal" runs the risk of being out of touch with teenagers today. Sure, we remember significant moments or can still feel our best and worst experiences, but most adults forget what it's really like to be a teenager. So when we had a younger youth leader in our Sticky Faith Innovation research—20-year-old Anna, a sophomore in college—we wanted to hear her interpretations of her own teenage search for identity, belonging, and purpose growing up. Here's a snapshot of the conversation:

ANNA: When I was in elementary and middle school, my identity and belonging were all found through dance. Whether somebody had known me for a really long time or they had just met me in the grocery store, I needed them to know, "I'm a dancer." But in my junior year of high school, I started taking dance with a teacher named Ms. Ann. She helped me realize that making dance my whole life came with a lot of issues.

FYI: How did she do that?

ANNA: Well, in nice and subtle ways, she helped me realize that my technical skills weren't good enough to be a professional dancer. But there was also a point when my family was going through something difficult, and she could tell I was struggling but didn't want to show it. She took me aside during a dance practice and told me, "You know, it's okay to not be okay." And I began to understand that all of my perfectionism around dance and in every area of life was really toxic. Ms. Ann helped me see that dance could be a wonderful part of my life, but it didn't have to be my entire life. She opened a door for me to ask the questions of identity, belonging, and purpose again and to seek out God's better answers—answers that are shaped by Jesus' grace and love.

Remember, in Chapter 1 we introduced the questions of identity, belonging, and purpose that all people, but especially teenagers, are asking. Head on back to pages 23 to 24 if you need a refresher on the full explanation.

We're struck by how Anna is able to look back and reflect on her own teenage journey, using identity, belonging, and purpose as categories to make sense of her experiences. And we're inspired by her mentor. Ms. Ann had the ability to empathize with Anna, name the message Anna felt caught up in, and offer her a better, alternative story that helped set Anna free.

We would like all of our teenagers to end up as thoughtful as Anna. But Annas need Anns. What we really need is to be like Ms. Ann and equip our volunteer teams to be like her too.

Interpreting: making sense of teenagers' lives

In previous chapters, we explained how young people's everyday instabilities raise questions of who they are, where they fit, and the difference they can make in the world. It is in these unstable spaces and in teenagers' searches for new answers that they need the support of youth leaders and youth ministry most.

For Sticky Faith Innovation, **interpreting** *means making sense of two things in particular: what you heard when you empathized with your teenagers in the first innovation step, and how the gospel matters to young people's everyday instabilities and searches for identity, belonging, and purpose.*

Interpreting what your teenagers share with you empowers you to step closer to their lives, help them reflect on their experiences, and point them toward God's better answers.

But what do we mean by "interpreting"?

To interpret is to *make sense of something*. As humans, we interpret all the time. Whether at church, home, or online, we're constantly bombarded with new information, experiences, and stories that we have to somehow comprehend. For Sticky Faith Innovation, interpreting means making sense of two things in particular: what you heard when you empathized with your teenagers in the first innovation step, and how the gospel matters to young people's everyday instabilities and searches for identity, belonging, and purpose.

What support can youth ministry offer young people like teenage Anna, who was finding her whole worth in dance? Or students like Anthony, whose parents are divorcing, or teenagers like Gabriel, who seem to only care about getting into a top college?

By interpreting what teenagers share with you, you can begin to discover their current answers to identity, belonging, and purpose, and God's better answers. The more we understand teenagers' stories and what their stories mean to them, the better chance we have of connecting the good news Jesus offers with their everyday experiences.

Current answers: the answers teenagers have now

Young people consider multiple messages as they seek answers to their questions of identity, belonging, and purpose. These messages might originate from movies, social media, teachers, church leaders, peers, parents, or themselves. The ones young people come to believe are their *current answers* to who they are, where they fit, and the difference they can make in the world.

Definitions:

Current answers *are the messages and stories teenagers believe that shape how they see themselves (identity), their connections to others (belonging), and their contributions to the world (purpose).*

Jesus-centered answers *are the truths God invites teenagers to live into concerning who they are (identity), their connections to others (belonging), and their contributions to the world (purpose).*

Teenagers' current answers can be good, bad, contradictory, heartfelt, confusing, and evolving. And those current answers sometimes serve them well; but often, they fail them.

When young people's current answers come up short, they start searching for better ones. As youth leaders, our job is to compassionately discern our students' current answers so we can help them find the better, more *Jesus-centered answers* God offers them. The better you interpret teenagers' current and Jesus-centered answers, the more "Ms. Ann-like" moments you can have with your students. We all want that!

The great news is that you're on your way. The *compassion* move you've started, by empathizing with your teenagers, sets you up to really listen to your individual students and help them begin making sense of the current answers they're holding.

In the how-to exercises of Chapter 3, your innovation team looked for common themes that began to give you insight into your students' collective current answers. In other words, there may be threads that weave through all your conversations with teenagers in your community, revealing similar fears, questions, hopes, aspirations, or longings. Perhaps there has even been an event in your community that has impacted and shaped many of them.

Capturing these themes sets you up to begin interpreting what they mean for your young people by using the categories of identity, belonging, and purpose. Now you can discern what your young people are really seeking after, hurting from, and hoping for (see the how-to exercises at the end of this chapter for a step-by-step guide). For example, youth leaders from our Sticky Faith Innovation research project interpreted the collective current answers of the young people that make up each of their youth groups. As they listened to diverse young people in their communities, certain threads seemed to connect all of their teenagers' stories. Read these real examples we share below slowly. Let each phrase sink in—they are quite moving. Picture your own teenagers saying some of these statements about themselves as they search for their true identity, belonging, and purpose.[19]

Identity – Who am I?

"I'm relational, hard-working, and compassionate."
"I'm not enough."
"My identity is too fragile, so I need to hide it from others and God."

Belonging – Where do I fit?

"If I can be my real self with you, then we'll be close."
"I'm so alone, I don't feel anymore."
"If you really knew me, you wouldn't accept or love me, because your love is conditional."

Purpose – How can my life matter?

"I think I know what I want to do in life, but I'm not sure it has anything to do with God."
"I am what I do."
"I am a performer in a story I have no power to control."

Read those current answers again. Leaders found that these "stories behind the stories" capture why many of their young people engage, disengage, perform, or act out. Discovering their teenagers' current answers strengthened these leaders' ministries in three crucial ways.

First, as we mentioned before, their teenagers gained an adult who could help them better understand their own experiences. One youth leader, Miguel, and his innovation team discerned this current answer: "I have to perform to be accepted, and I'm the only one who feels like this." Just a week later, one of Miguel's students vented to him about how worn out she was from her studies. Miguel listened intently and empathetically responded, "It sounds like you feel like you have to perform to be accepted." She looked up at Miguel wide-eyed and simply said, *"Yeah."* In that moment, she felt seen and understood. When you interpret what you hear from young people well, you can give language to teenagers' deepest struggles.

Second, by discerning their teenagers' current answers, these youth leaders were able to uncover why some of their youth ministry talks, programs, and events may not have yielded the kinds of results they hoped for. Some of their ministry programming failed to engage teenagers' current answers to their biggest questions. Discerning your students' current answers can take some of the mystery out of why some aspects of your ministry thrive while others flounder.

Third, and most importantly in the Sticky Faith Innovation process, discerning their teenagers' current answers to identity, belonging, and purpose provided greater focus for their future innovative efforts. Each youth leader arrived at a simple, concise, and powerful statement that captured the core of their teenagers' searches for identity, belonging, and purpose. Interpreting your young people's current answers can focus your ministry and all of your innovative efforts to support teenagers where they need you most. And when leaders can name their teenagers' current answers, they have a solid starting point to introduce them to better, more Jesus-centered answers.

Jesus-centered answers: the answers teenagers are searching for

We all want young people to trust Jesus with their lives both now and in the future, which means we must invite teenagers to live into a gospel that responds to their everyday instabilities and quests for identity, belonging, and purpose. We also believe teenagers want these answers too. Finding them is part of their spiritual journey and a faith that sticks.

Jesus-centered answers to identity, belonging, and purpose point teenagers to the good news of the gospel. They respond to what teenagers search for and give them a vision for who they can become. And they tell young people good news, just in time—like Anna, who needed to hear that, "It's okay to not be okay." Jesus-centered answers invite young people to find their whole selves in God.

In the how-to exercises at the end of this chapter, we provide you with step-by-step instructions for discerning Jesus-centered answers that connect with your teenagers' current answers. But before you get there, listen to some of the Jesus-centered answers leaders from our Sticky Faith Innovation research project came up with. Listen especially for the just-in-time good news.

CURRENT ANSWER ⟶ JESUS-CENTERED ANSWER

Identity – Who am I?

"My identity is too fragile, so ⟶ "Jesus knows me and I need to hide it from others chooses me, and my story and God." matters in God's story and is worth sharing."

Belonging – Where do I fit?

"I'm so alone, I don't feel ⟶ "In Jesus and my church anymore." community, I am fully known and *still* loved!"

Purpose – How can I make a difference?

"I am a performer in a story I ⟶ "I am a masterpiece created have no power to control." in the image of God and have a unique role in God's great story."

—*Current and Jesus-centered answers developed by youth leaders from the Sticky Faith Innovation research project*

If you heard your teenagers saying one of these Jesus-centered answers about themselves, wouldn't it sound like good news? By discerning these better answers to their teenagers' deepest questions, these leaders raised the quality of their ministries and focused their innovative work in three important ways.

First, this work helped them articulate how the gospel intersects with their teenagers' everyday lives in the present and is big enough to direct their lives in the future. Jesus' call to follow him is an invitation to teenagers to find out who they truly are, where they fit, and the difference they can make in the world and the lives of others. It's a call that can stick with them at ages 15, 35, and 75.

Second, by interpreting Jesus-centered answers, these youth leaders discerned a theological goal, a telos, that guided their future ministry energy and efforts. Their goal was that their teenagers might discover these answers for themselves. You can know your young people are grasping the good news of the gospel for their lives when you hear them vocalizing (without prompting) Jesus-centered answers about themselves and their peers, you notice them befriending those who are not like them, or you see them making sacrifices for a cause that is bigger than themselves.

Third, when you interpret teenagers' current and Jesus-centered answers, you can begin to see the gap between the two—the gap between the answers that currently define teenagers' identity, belonging, and purpose and the good news answers that could. Bridging this gap is what Sticky Faith Innovation is all about.

Youth ministry is meant for this gap.

You are called to this gap.

The gap: where youth leaders go

There is a gap between the lives teenagers experience and the full life Jesus desires for them. Sometimes this gap feels dramatically wide as teenagers navigate crises, mistakes, or disappointments. Other times the gap may narrow as young people encounter God in their instabilities, they taste joy, or they feel connected to a greater purpose.

The gap is where teenagers feel the instability in their lives, and it is in this space that they search for better answers to their questions of identity, belonging, and purpose.

Remember, your job isn't to resolve the complexity of teenagers' lives or offer quick fixes. Instead, you and your fellow leaders are called to accompany young people as they travel from their current answers to the Jesus-centered answers that can bring them life—to let them know, "It's okay to not be okay. I'm right here with you."

As you step into the gap with teenagers, remember these important truths:

The gap is real

The tensions and struggles young people experience are more than them "just being teenagers" who will eventually "grow out of it." They are trying to navigate confusing worlds in which their understandings of God and themselves are often challenged and few certainties remain. Doubts, questions, and searching are necessary for long-term faith, and leaders can support teenagers' journeys toward a faith that sticks by making space for them.

The gap is not between teenagers and God

Let's make something clear: The gap teenagers experience does not mean God is far away. A youth leaders' job is to help teenagers become aware of God's presence in every circumstance, every laugh, every tear, and every longing. God is always with young people in their journeys from their current to Jesus-centered answers. The honor and challenge for youth leaders and their teams is to step closer to teenagers in the gaps where God is already present, and to accompany them on their journeys.

Youth ministry can help bridge the gap

As a youth leader, you are called by God to help bridge this gap between teenagers' current and Jesus-centered answers—to help them hear and internalize the messages that can offer them hope and ultimately set them free.

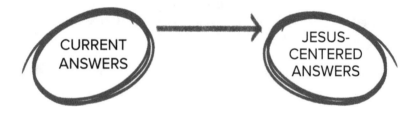

We know it is in these gaps that youth leaders' hearts weep, fear, and cheer—hoping that their ministries might help teenagers find more Jesus-centered answers that can respond to their everyday lives and be big enough to guide them into the future. By identifying the gap, you can know where to focus your innovative efforts.

Before you move on to the next chapter to imagine fresh ways of supporting your teenagers' searches for identity, belonging, and purpose, we encourage you to pray.

Pray for your young people

God, may the teenagers in our community sense your presence as they search for their true identity, belonging, and purpose. May they know they are not alone.

Pray for yourselves

Lord, the gap between teenagers' current lives and the lives you desire for them sometimes feels so wide. Please help me feel your presence as I stand with young people in the gap.

Pray for your community

Lord, please raise up more adults who can stand in the gap with our teenagers. Give our church creativity as we seek to accompany young people on their journeys toward more life-giving answers to who they are, where they fit, and the difference they can make in the world.

Amen.

REFLECT

1. When you look at the examples of teenagers' current answers on page 87, which ones align most with your young people? In what ways are young people in your community different from the examples provided?

STICKY FAITH **INNOVATION**

REFLECT

2. What do you think prevents teenagers in your
   community from believing and living out of
   more Jesus-centered answers?

REFLECT

3. We all wrestle with various messages about our identity, belonging, and purpose. What messages might you be wrestling with, and what Jesus-centered answers might God be calling you to find in your own faith journey?

HOW-TO EXERCISES FOR INTERPRETING

These how-to exercises guide you in interpreting the messages that shape your teenagers' current answers to their questions of identity, belonging, and purpose and the Jesus-centered answers they're searching for. Be sure to complete Chapter 3's how-to exercises before moving on to this step. We suggest that you schedule one to two meetings with your innovation team to work through these exercises together.

These how-to exercises will guide you to accomplish the following:

1. Your innovation team will sort your listening notes and themes by the categories of identity, belonging, and purpose, and summarize a current answer for each.

2. Your innovation team will reflect on the current answers and envision what Jesus might speak to your young people as an alternative answer that is good news for them.

3. Lastly, you will create a "gap sentence" that summarizes a current answer your young people hold and a Jesus-centered answer that promises better news. This gap is where you will focus your innovation work in future chapters.

Current answers

Interpret your listening notes and themes to discover your teenagers' current answers to identity, belonging, and purpose.

As a team, discuss:

1. In light of your listening notes and themes, how do you see teenagers in your community answering their questions of identity, belonging, and purpose right now?

    a. Who am I?

    b. Where do I fit?

    c. What difference can I make?

Use the following chart to help guide your processing:

IDENTITY	BELONGING	PURPOSE
Who am I?	Where do I fit?	What difference can I make?
How do these teenagers describe themselves? What labels or characteristics do they use to portray who they are?	How do these teenagers describe their relationships to others and to their communities? Who do they trust or where do they feel most connected?	How do these teenagers describe their personal goals and aspirations? How do they make meaning of what they're doing right now?

2. In addition to how teenagers are answering their questions of identity, belonging, and purpose, what other themes stand out? What important observations do you want to keep in mind or not lose sight of?

3. Now, attempt to summarize teenagers' current answers from the perspective of teenagers ("I ... "), in 1–3 sentences. You may wish to focus on identity, belonging, or purpose, or a compilation of all three. See page 87 for examples from other youth leaders who have gone through this process before.

4. Compare this current answer with your listening notes and themes. Does it faithfully capture what you heard? Does it get a layer deeper to the instabilities teenagers experience regarding their searches for their true identity, belonging, and purpose?

Jesus-centered answers

Articulate what it sounds like for a young person to embrace Jesus' loving invitation, "Come, follow me," as they seek their true identity, belonging, and purpose.

As a team:

1. Start by rereading the current answer you articulated as an innovation team. As you empathize with your teenagers' searches for identity, belonging, and purpose more deeply, what comes to mind about the new answers you hope teenagers will discover for themselves?

2. Take some time to imagine Jesus responding directly to the teenagers you interviewed. In Scripture, how did Jesus respond to people who came to him? When did he respond in compassion, healing, rebuke, or prophetic authority? What do you imagine Jesus might say in response to your teenagers' deepest questions around their identity, belonging, and purpose?

3. Write the new answer you hope teenagers will live into—a Jesus-centered answer shaped by the love of Jesus and the story of God. Start with each of the prompts below. You might find it helpful to explore Scripture passages that come to mind, and you might find other images that help bridge teenagers' current answers with Jesus-centered answers. [You may want to start this reflection individually and then share with each other as a team.]

Who am I? (Identity)

I am ...

Where do I fit? (Belonging)

I belong ...

What difference can I make? (Purpose)

I can ...

4. Together as a team, write a Jesus-centered answer that responds to the current answer you wrote above, in 1–3 sentences. What would it sound like for a young person to have their answers to identity, belonging, and purpose shaped by the love of Jesus and the story of God? This Jesus-centered answer will likely be a compilation of your answers in question 3 of Jesus-centered answers. Articulate it in the first person, from the perspective of a teenager ("I ...)

Current Answer   Jesus-centered answer

_____   _____

_____   _____

_____   _____

5. Reread the current answer and the Jesus-centered answer you've articulated. Does the Jesus-centered answer sound like good news to teenagers in your community? Does it acknowledge (rather than deny) the reality of young people's current answers while simultaneously calling them into a new one?

6. Now, summarize the work you've done and the work you have yet to do by filling in the blanks of this gap sentence:

Gap Sentence:
Because our teenagers feel/believe
" _____ "
[current answer]

We will innovate_____
[leave this blank for now. This is the work of the creativity move!]

In order that young people might believe/discover
" _____ "
[Jesus-centered answer].

This gap sentence will be your compass as you start the expanding step in the next chapter. It summarizes whom you serve, what they need, and how you might eventually seek to bridge the gap.

Share your findings with your discernment team

Now that you have turned your empathy and listening into current and Jesus-centered answers, share these messages and your gap sentence with your discernment team. Explain that these answers summarize what you have heard from young people and what you believe God desires for them. Ask your discernment team to pray for your students and your efforts to bridge the gap between their current and Jesus-centered answers.

Now

You are understanding the deeper struggles of the teenagers you serve.

You are advocating for them by empathizing with them and inviting other adults to do the same through sharing their current and Jesus-centered answers.

You are ready to expand your ministry imaginations.

CREATIVITY

We dare to reach beyond the safe
and familiar,
By expanding our imaginations,
And narrowing our focus,
To do whatever it takes to support young
people where they need us most.

"What shall we say the kingdom of God
is like, or what parable shall we use to
describe it? It is like a mustard seed,
which is the smallest of all seeds on
earth. Yet when planted, it grows and
becomes the largest of all garden plants,
with such big branches that the birds
can perch in its shade."

—Mark 4:30–32

CHAPTER FIVE

Expand Your Ministry Imaginations: Creating Possibilities that Can Bridge the Gap

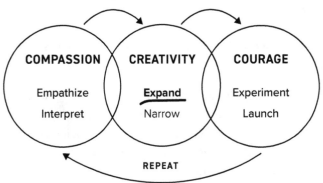

The Sticky Faith Innovation Process

Expanding helped our team realize that we were actually being creative! We were trusting each other enough to bring our ideas.

—Bianca, youth leader

We asked a youth leader in our Sticky Faith Innovation research project to reflect on the new ministry approach she and her team developed, and how well she thought their approach went. Irene put it this way:

> I felt like our team learned how to make informed decisions on how we can serve our teens. We focused our work on learning to listen and tell our own faith and life stories and, after talking with our students and volunteers, they said we "nailed it" with what they needed.

"You nailed it."

Youth leaders would love to hear that from teenagers every time.

What we love about Irene's reflection is that what her team "nailed" wasn't a perfect program (they shared plenty of mistakes) or that it addressed every challenge their students faced (it didn't and it raised a few more), but that her teenagers said their new approach connected with them, helped them, and encouraged them.

Irene's team did the important, innovative work you're attempting.

With each step of the Sticky Faith Innovation process, we're setting you up to support your teenagers where they need you most. Instead of relying on enthusiasm, panic, or guessing, you're ready to do what Irene's youth ministry did— make a purposeful and compassionate attempt to serve your teenagers where they need you most. Or as their students affirmed, "Nail it."

While *compassion* grounds your innovation, it also leads you to the next crucial move in Sticky Faith Innovation—*creativity*. *Creativity* calls for two key steps: *expanding* and *narrowing*.

These steps are designed to channel your compassion to tap into your creativity as you support young people in the gap. In this chapter on expanding, we'll guide you in stretching your ministry imaginations to revolutionize your brainstorming, multiply your options, and encourage you and your team to create again.

Expanding your ideas

We think youth leaders are some of the most creative people we know. Still, even youth workers retreat to safe and familiar ministry methods to avoid risk and reduce anxiety. Our inner critical voices sound the alarm:

What if I'm not that creative?

What if my new ideas fail?

How will those who like the old ways react?

How do I justify new approaches to my leadership?

Is it worth it?

Questions like these haunt every leader who entertains the thought of changing their approach or trying something new. The great news is that expanding prepares you and your team to stretch your imaginations—tapping into your creativity in order to think of new ways to communicate Jesus-centered answers that speak to the gap you have identified.

All leaders can get stuck in predictable patterns that limit their problem solving. We discovered from our innovation research that many of us often default to "what we've done in the past," which can inhibit our creative process. Expanding asks us to leave that phrase behind!

This step of expanding your imaginations also frees you and

your team to realize that you have more potential for new ideas than you realize. You just have to believe it and rewire some of the ways you view your ministry. We've discovered that leaders were more prepared to innovate when they realized the following truths about creativity.

No idea is a bad idea (honest)

You've certainly heard this phrase, "No idea is a bad idea," offered at the beginning of a brainstorming meeting. Then, someone says something utterly ridiculous and you've muttered to yourself, "That actually was a bad idea."

No one wants to be the "bad idea" person. Fear of being the bad-idea person makes brainstorming meetings awkward, predictable, noninspiring sessions that accomplish little more than rehashing old, familiar, safe ideas that rarely inspire and are eventually forgotten. Brainstorming sessions can be better than that. Expanding involves exercises designed to release you and your team from worrying about whether they are offering "good" or "bad" ideas—freeing you to think creatively in a judgment-free, trust-building environment.

More ideas are better than one good idea

Not only do leaders worry about coming up with bad ideas, but we also witnessed many only trying to come up with that one, killer idea. As a result, they got stuck, hyper focused on trying to create one "game-changing" idea to solve every problem. Expanding removes the pressure to find one solution and provides the freedom for your team to play with many diverse ideas. This may sound counterintuitive, but we have learned from leading innovation experts that when teams are free to create lots of ideas, they end up generating more quality solutions than teams who try to get one attempt right the first time. Get ready to generate lots of ideas![20]

Your limitations are your friends

Some youth leaders we worked with thought they couldn't be creative because they felt limited by what their youth ministry, church, or community *didn't* have. Their lack of money, facilities, resources, leaders—you name it—acted like a wet blanket for any of their innovative sparks. Certainly, no youth ministry has unlimited resources, but here's the great news—your limitations can actually inspire your innovation, not dampen it.

Think about art. Every painting has an edge, and the painter must work within the space afforded. The artist must push herself to portray color, emotion, and message all within the frame. No space is wasted, every brushstroke counts. Some artists even limit themselves to a restricted color palette from which to create. Masterpieces are made here.

Or consider technology, where engineers must make components faster and smaller to produce devices that are enjoyable and useful. Small phones have transformed the way we access information and communicate. Or think about those moments when your refrigerator looked empty, but you took limited ingredients and created an amazing meal that is now a household favorite!

Constraints force our creativity. They are not barriers, only boundaries pushing you to innovate what could be your next youth ministry masterpiece.

Your community has more assets than you think

Expanding also helped youth leaders in our work realize they had more assets than they thought. Many discovered unused spaces, generous donors, interested senior citizens, enthusiastic business owners, local artists, and new community partnerships. These resources and relationships stretched their imaginations for new ministry possibilities with teenagers. We think your community assets are waiting to be discovered by you too.[21] What people, resources, experiences, locations, neighbors, families, friendships, skills, traditions, or talents are in your midst? Perhaps more than you've noticed because they're outside the bounds of what you usually count.

God's creativity inspires our creativity

Let's remember that creativity isn't a special gift for a few but is inspired by God for all. God's creativity bursts onto the scene in Genesis 1. Even after the fall in Genesis 3, we see God's commitment to restoring and healing humanity, often in surprisingly creative ways. Further, Jesus' life and teachings call his followers to reimagine the kingdom of God with his mantra, "You have heard it said ... but I tell you ..." (Matthew 5). And the church, birthed by the Spirit, continues to live out the good news by seeking to care for each other, live in harmony with one another, and serve their neighbors—hoping for a better world (Acts 2, Revelation 21). God invites us, as image-bearers of a Creator-God, to use our gifts and stories to join in creatively loving and healing the world through the power of God's Spirit (John 20:21–22). Your creativity has a supernatural source. Exercising it is an act of faith and an expression of worship.

Expanding toward the gap

Once we embrace our expanding potential, we can direct our creative energies toward the gap where our teenagers need us most.

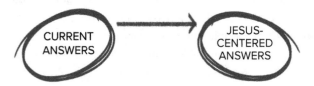

There's a good chance that this gap is not completely new to you. You may already have ministry programs in place that intend to bridge the gap, but you may also be discovering that they are not working as well as you intended or your ministry could be doing more. Through expanding, you can revisit your current programming or even try something new. Your focus is on bridging the gap—the places where your teenagers are searching and the spaces where they need you most.

Expanding purposeful programs and portable practices

We propose that leaders who bridge the gap are those who can innovate and reimagine their programs and practices to provide teenagers with the spiritual support they need. We'll explain what we mean by "programs" and "practices" below, but we offer this crucial perspective first—young people's faith does not stick for the long-term through us giving them information alone. They need environments where they can practice their faith—programs. And not just any programs—programs built for them, not for us. Further, they need portable Christian practices to develop spiritual habits that they can take with them wherever they go.

Purposeful programs

Many youth leaders admit that their ministry programs can lose their sense of purpose and can even become obstacles to supporting teenagers in the gaps where they need the church most. When programs fail to point teenagers to Jesus-centered answers or offer adult accompaniment on their faith journeys, young people see them merely as extra-curricular activities or clean, optional fun that only matter when their other essential life-pressures are managed.

Your youth ministry programs have the potential to create climates where teenagers can wrestle with the gaps they feel between the messages they tell themselves and the promises God offers. This *creativity* step of expanding gives you and your team the opportunity to repurpose your youth ministry programs and even develop new ones.

To start, you may want to consider the programs you currently have or are considering building. A great exercise would be for you to list your programs and then ask, "What are these programs intending to accomplish?" Use the categories of identity, belonging, and purpose to gain clarity. See the chart on pages 118-119 for an example of programs that focus on identity, belonging, and purpose.

Your youth ministry programs have the potential to create climates where teenagers can wrestle with the gaps they feel between the messages they tell themselves and the promises God offers.

What teenagers are searching for:

	IDENTITY	BELONGING	PURPOSE
KEY QUESTION	Who am I?	Where do I fit?	What difference can I make?
DESCRIPTION	Young people's view of themselves	Young people's connections to others	Young people's contributions to the world

What are our programs intending to accomplish?

PROGRAMS	Teenagers' search for...
	IDENTITY
MIDWEEK GATHERING	
WEEKEND MORNING CLASS	We teach about what it means to be Christian.
WEEKEND SERVICES	
MENTORING	We offer support and guidance to help young people know themselves.
MISSION TRIPS	We encourage teenagers to reach out to others to learn from them and more about themselves.
TRANSITIONS/MILESTONES	
CAMPS	We create time and environments for teenagers to grow with God.
SMALL GROUPS	
ONLINE INTERACTION	
LEADERSHIP TEAMS	
THE ARTS	We value what teenagers are good at in all forms.
CAUSES	
NEW PROGRAM	

STICKY FAITH **INNOVATION**

Teenagers' search for...

BELONGING	PURPOSE
We provide community, friendship, and support.	
We encourage intergenerational connection.	We model how we worship together.
	We promote serving others.
Our community sends, welcomes, and supports young people.	
We provide extended time and experiences for young people to connect and grow together.	
We encourage deep, meaningful, spiritual friendships.	
We seek to offer dialogue and support throughout the week, outside the church.	
	We promote servant leadership.
	We encourage justice and activism.

What are our programs intending to accomplish? Notice that every program doesn't resolve every search your teenagers have. Also, recognize that you may discover that what your program intends to do might not be accomplishing your goals. A balcony view like this one may help you identify a particular program you might want to reimagine to better address the gap you have identified.

Now, let's consider Irene's youth ministry for a moment. Through their compassionate work of empathizing and interpreting, her team realized that their teenagers felt like they needed to be perfect for their peers, parents, teachers, and youth leaders, which was creating tremendous anxiety over an impossible goal. Irene's team determined that this current answer distorted their students' search for identity. Let's say that the chart on the prior page described their current programming: If they wanted to help teenagers find a more hopeful and healthier Jesus-centered answer, they could start with one of the programs they already have and innovate within it to address the gap. For example, they could reimagine their approach to mentoring, their summer camp, or how they incorporate the arts in their youth ministry. Yet another youth leader going through this process might realize they don't have a mentoring program and need to start from scratch. This innovative process could help that leader create a mentoring program that doesn't yet exist. Expanding helps you reimagine a program to make it more purposeful or to make it possible.

Portable practices

Our original Sticky Faith research reported that many committed, church-attending young people become disconnected from the church once they graduate.[22] One of the challenges graduating seniors face is that they can't take their youth ministry with them. Youth leaders believe their role is to prepare young people for lifelong faith. Faith that lasts requires practice. And Christian practices can be the portable disciplines that call young people to Jesus-centered answers and continue to transform their lives well beyond high school.

Christian practices support a growing, maturing faith by instilling a Jesus-centered vision of identity, belonging, and purpose. Through practices, the Spirit shapes our faith communities and forms us as individuals. Think of practices as rituals and habits that teenagers share with their faith community wherever they are and wherever they go.

Working from this understanding of practices in our Sticky Faith Innovation research, we honed in on lament, testimony, Sabbath, hospitality, vocation, and justice. We envisioned how reimagining these historic Christian practices might meet teenagers in the current gaps they experience. Here are a few examples:

THE PRACTICE OF TESTIMONY

Testimony is about learning how to share and listen to the life and faith stories that are important to us and others. Shared stories may support your teenagers' search for identity.

Your youth ministry may want to reimagine ways to share testimonies when you notice a gap where:

- You sense that your teenagers need a clearer picture of how their own life stories and identities connect with God's story.

- You realize your young people need opportunities to express the hope and grief in their lives.

- You recognize that your students struggle with sharing their beliefs and doubts, and you want to encourage them to be their authentic selves.

THE PRACTICE OF HOSPITALITY

Christian hospitality is about how we make relational room for each other as God makes room for us. At times, we all feel on the "outside" and need to feel welcomed. This practice may address young peoples' search for belonging.

Your youth ministry may want to create ways to practice hospitality when you notice a gap where:

Christian practices are rituals and habits that teenagers share with their faith community wherever they are and wherever they go.

- Your teenagers are unwilling or unable to reach out to others beyond their familiar friendships.

- You see or hear teenagers say they feel alone or unwelcome.

- Your group finds it hard to trust each other because they rarely interact with each other or don't have opportunities for meaningful engagement.

Notice how we have approached these practices. Their purpose is to shape teenagers' searches for identity, belonging, and purpose. Perhaps the gap you have identified does not need a new program but an approach that encourages your young people to practice their faith both in and outside your youth ministry. By expanding your imaginations for what's possible in your ministry, you can innovate new ways to encourage teenagers to practice their faith to help bridge the gap between their current and Jesus-centered answers.

Again, let's take Irene's youth ministry as an example. Her innovation team reimagined the practice of testimony in ways that didn't require teenagers' stories to have happy endings. Their expanding work ultimately led them to create space for young people to testify about the hopeful, hard, even tragic parts of their lives. Students wrote their stories and posted them where other church members could read them. Adults in the congregation then placed a dot sticker on all of the stories they related to, demonstrating solidarity with each young person's story. Irene's innovation team expanded what "testimony" meant, helping young people share their stories and know that they are not alone in the church.

Both programs and practices are great places to focus your innovation. The expanding exercises in the how-to section at the end of this chapter will open up new ways to support your teenagers through programs and practices.

———————————

In our Sticky Faith Innovation research, we found that youth leaders who reimagined Christian practices in ways that were participatory, ongoing, both personal and communal, and gradual had the most success in helping their teenagers discover more Jesus-centered answers.

- Participatory: Young people were active participants, rather than passive observers.

- Ongoing: Practices threaded throughout the life of the church, rather than being reimagined solely as one-time events (faith formation takes time!).

- Personal and Communal: Young people learned how to practice their faith as they gathered with other believers, and they learned to engage in the reimagined practice on their own, as well.

- Gradual: Youth leaders created ways to pace participation, which helped teenagers grow in the practice over time.[23]

Getting started with expanding

So let's pull together what we've highlighted above. First, recognize that you have the potential to expand your ministry innovations. Don't let the past, your fears, or your limitations keep you from seeing the potential in what you and your team can do. Second, expand toward the gap. Focus on what you discovered your teenagers need most from you. Take one challenge at a time. Third, name the programs and practices you can imagine and reimagine that can address the gap and serve your young people.

And fourth, stay focused. Your Sticky Faith Innovation work so far has already set you up for this. Practically, we discovered that youth leaders stayed focused on their innovation when they could easily explain what they were doing. You already have the elements for the gap sentence that you and your leaders can use from the how-to exercises in the previous chapter. Now you can start filling in the middle "program or practice" blank:

Because our teenagers feel/believe
"_____" *[current answer]*

We will innovate _____
[selected program area or practice]

In order that young people might believe/discover
"_____"
[Jesus-centered answer].

Let's offer a final example from Irene's ministry. Prior to developing their innovative approach to testimony (which we describe above), they used this statement to fuel as many ideas as possible to bridge the gap:

Because our teenagers believe, "I have to be perfect or at least look like it" [current answer]

We will innovate a way for teenagers to practice testimony to give them opportunities to talk about their lives, faith, doubt, mistakes, and hopes with each other in a safe and supportive environment [practice/program]

In order that our young people might know, "Even though I am not perfect, God loves me perfectly" [Jesus-centered answer].

A gap sentence like this can set you up to expand, as well. It keeps you focused on bridging the gap, providing direction for the new program or practice you hope to innovate.

Now it is time to turn toward expanding in the how-to exercises below that provide you with step-by-step instructions to help you and your team expand your imaginations and develop your new, and even out of the blue, ideas. This is your opportunity to translate your compassion into creativity.

REFLECT

1. How comfortable do you and your team feel about sharing your ideas with each other? To expand well, you and your team need to trust each other. What are the strengths and challenges of your team right now? How will you foster trust and freedom to create together?

REFLECT

2. What do you see as your faith community's assets and limitations? Remember that both can encourage your innovation.

HOW-TO EXERCISES FOR EXPANDING

In this section, we prepare you for your creativity move by taking your innovation team through the process of expanding upon a program area or practice that you believe can help your teenagers begin to move from their current answer to a more Jesus-centered answer. For this work, we suggest that you schedule two 90-minute meetings with your team.

By following these how-to exercises on expanding, you will:

1. Decide on a program or practice you desire to innovate around and a gap sentence that will allow you to focus your expanding efforts.

2. Do expanding exercises as a team to give you some great possibilities for how you might innovate in the gap.

3. Discover a new way to generate creative ideas, while bonding as a team.

Expanding together

Our research has revealed that the best ideas rarely emerge from one person, but rather through your shared work together. Recognize that each member on your innovation team may have a different reaction to expanding. Some are natural "expanders" who love to think of new ideas, keep their options open, and change course as quickly as possible. Others on your team may be less enthusiastic about expanding. They are the realists, the pragmatists, the ones who want a clear plan, low risk, and defined outcomes. They'll shine during the next creative step—narrowing your best ideas. For now, expanding invites your whole innovation team to step out of their comfort zones and create together. This is the space to stretch your imaginations with the hopes of capturing something new, inspiring, and hopeful.

Prepare to expand! (Meeting 1)

In your first meeting, your team will work together to decide what program or practice you might try to innovate to bridge the gap between your teenagers' current answers and the hopeful, Jesus-centered answers the gospel offers.

Programs Exercise

To help you focus your efforts, invite your team to fill out the following program table to identify how your current offerings speak to teenagers' quests for identity, belonging, and purpose. List what you have. Don't expect to fill out the whole chart, as you may not have some of the program examples offered.

In this chart, answer: What are our programs intending to accomplish?

PROGRAMS	Teenagers' search for...
	IDENTITY
MIDWEEK GATHERING	
WEEKEND MORNING CLASS	
WEEKEND SERVICES	
MENTORING	
MISSION TRIPS	
TRANSITIONS/MILESTONES	
CAMPS	
SMALL GROUPS	
ONLINE INTERACTION	
LEADERSHIP TEAMS	
THE ARTS	
CAUSES	
NEW PROGRAM	

Teenagers' search for...

BELONGING	PURPOSE

What areas are missing that you might want to innovate around and that can help bridge the gap your team has identified?

Practice exercise

Another route is for your team to consider Christian practices that might help bridge the gap between your teenagers' current and Jesus-centered answers. While this list isn't comprehensive, it can help you start considering what your ministry currently offers and areas that could use some innovation. In the chart that follows, identify how you currently engage teenagers in your ministry in each practice and how this engagement speaks to teenagers' quests for identity, belonging, and purpose.

In this chart, answer: How do teenagers in our ministry engage in each practice, and how might their participation speak to their searches for identity, belonging, and purpose?

What areas are missing that you might want to innovate around and that can help bridge the gap your team has identified? What practices might your church engage with, but in a very limited way and that could use some reimagining?

PRACTICES	Teenagers' search for...		
	IDENTITY	BELONGING	PURPOSE
TESTIMONY			
LAMENT			
SABBATH			
HOSPITALITY			
VOCATION/ CALLING			
JUSTICE AND MERCY			
WORSHIP			
SCRIPTURE STUDY AND MEDITATION			
OTHER PRACTICES			

You can complete either or both charts depending on the direction your team feels led to go. Discuss as a team which area you would like to focus on innovating. But do not get tripped up into thinking that there is only one right program area or practice. Just start with one. You can always try another program or practice at another time.

Landing on a gap sentence

Together, as a team, decide on your best gap sentence. Ending your first expanding meeting this way will give your team focus and will be your starting point for your second expanding team meeting.

Gap Sentence:

Because our teenagers feel/believe " _____
_____ *" [current answer]*

We will innovate _____
[selected program area or practice]

In order that young people might believe/discover
" _____ *"*

[Jesus-centered answer].

Start expanding! (Meeting 2)

Now your innovation team is ready to creatively and intentionally brainstorm ways to innovate the program or practice you have chosen. We recommend that you follow these sub-steps:

Pray together

- Ask God to inspire your thinking, release you from fear, and help you to have fun!

Icebreaker

- Start out with a fun, risk-free exercise just to get everyone comfortable with being together. [For our favorite icebreaker and "expand" warm-up, we suggest playing the game Pictaphone.[24]]

Expand round 1: Brainwriting[25]

For this exercise, we suggest that you have 10 or more index cards per team member, pens, sticky notes, and dot stickers (optional).

1. *Generate Ideas* (Goal: Each team member writes as many ideas on separate index cards as possible in 7 minutes)

    a. Set a timer for 7 minutes and have each participant simultaneously:

    i. Take a stack of index cards.

    ii. Write out one idea per index card, with one to three sentences per card (making sure to write legibly). Each idea should attempt to bridge the gap between the current and Jesus-centered answers, as articulated in your gap sentence.

    iii. Pass filled-out index cards to the left and start on another idea on a new index card.

    iv. If participants get stuck, they can read through the index cards that have been passed to them to help spur their thinking (otherwise, there is no need to read each other's ideas at this stage).

    b. Stop after 7 minutes have passed.

    Expanding rule: Resist editing or revising your ideas.

Keep moving forward to the next one! You'll have plenty of time to develop your ideas later in the process.

2. *Organize the Chaos* (Goal: Organize all the ideas your team came up with)

    a. Have team members gather the cards they wrote their ideas on.

    b. Have each team member share their ideas out loud, while placing the corresponding index card on the table.

    c. Other members can add similar ideas to the ones shared.

    d. Eventually, your team will have stacks with unique ideas and some that are similar.

    e. After your team has organized your ideas by theme or category, label these stacks with a sticky note.

Expanding rule: No evaluating of ideas is allowed!

You're just organizing.

3. *Combine Ideas* (Goal: Come up with creative combinations)

    Some innovative ideas come from combining similar and different ideas. As a team, attempt to combine some of your ideas to come up with new ones. Write this new idea on a fresh card representing a combined idea.

Example: If one idea is to create a lament room where teenagers can express their anger and grief to God, and another idea is for leaders in the church to share their own stories of lament in a weekly vlog that teenagers can watch, combining these ideas might actually make for a more holistic and formative experience for participating teenagers and adults. Teenagers would see adults in the congregation modeling lament, and they would have space to practice lament as well.

4. *Save Your Best Ideas* (Goal: Each team member saves their favorite ideas from the whole team's pool of ideas, for future expanding)

   a. Saving your best ideas doesn't mean that your other ideas are "bad" or "wrong." It only means that you are trying to give your attention to a few ideas that show the most promise right now.

   b. In 5 minutes, each team member should take 3 dot stickers (or write your initials) and place them on their favorite ideas.

      Expanding rules:

      • No team discussion needs to happen here. This serves to give each team member a chance to save their favorites.

      • You are not deciding which idea your team will move forward with yet. Instead, you are indirectly weeding out any ideas your team finds less compelling.

   c. Any index card with a dot sticker (or initials) will move to the next stage.

Expand round 2: 6-minute turn

For this exercise, you will need: sticky notes, dot stickers (optional), pens, and a presentation-sized sticky note (optional)

1. *Build on one saved Brainwriting idea, 6 times in 6 minutes* (Goal: Expand on your saved ideas from the previous rounds to push your creative thinking)

   a. Have every team member choose 1 idea from your previous Brainwriting session (members might choose different ideas, but if some want to choose the same idea, that's fine, too).

   b. Each team member sets out 6 sticky notes on the space in front of them.

   c. Members will be given 1 minute per square to simultaneously expand on their chosen idea. The fast pace is designed to let your creative ideas emerge without overthinking them. Remember that the goal is more ideas, so don't worry about getting it "right."

      i. Team members can write a phrase, a few sentences, or draw a picture.

      ii. After each minute, team members will move to the next sticky note, expanding on that same Brainwriting idea in another way.

      iii. This is repeated until all 6 squares are filled (for a total of 6 minutes).

   d. Note: If a team member gets stuck with their chosen idea, they can feel free to switch to another saved Brainwriting idea.

Example: If a team member was building on the idea of a lament room, but was running out of ideas, the team member could switch to another saved idea (like a lament retreat) and complete the remaining minutes building on that idea.

2. *Organize the Chaos* (Goal: Organize all the ideas your team came up with)

   a. Now your team has come up with a lot of ideas that need organizing.

   b. Have each team member share their sticky note ideas, placing them on the table or presentation sized sticky note.

   c. Other members can add similar ideas to the ones shared to start organizing your team's ideas.

   d. Eventually, your team will have groups with unique ideas and some that are similar.

   e. After your team has organized your ideas by theme or category, label these clusters with a sticky note.

3. *Combine Ideas* (Goal: Come up with creative combinations)

   Some innovative ideas come from combining similar and different ideas. As a team, attempt to combine some of your ideas to come up with new ones. Write this new idea on a fresh card representing a combined idea.

4. *Save Your Best Ideas* (Goal: Each team member saves their favorite ideas from the whole team's pool of ideas)

   a. Like last time, remember that saving your best ideas

doesn't mean that your other ideas are "bad" or "wrong." It only means that you are trying to give your attention to a few ideas that show the most promise right now.

b. In 5 minutes, each team member should take 3 dot stickers (or write your initials) and place them on their favorite ideas.

Expanding rules:

- No team discussion needs to happen here. This serves to give each team member a chance to save their favorites.

- You are not deciding which idea your team will move forward with yet. Instead, you are indirectly weeding out any ideas your team finds less compelling.

c. Any index card with a dot sticker will move to the next creativity step—narrowing.

Drawing from your pool of ideas

Great job! You and your team have generated a whole lot of ideas and have chosen to expand some of them even further. Together, you have settled on a handful that everyone is favorable toward. And though some of you may have favorites, your collaboration in this process gives you room to hold your ideas as "our" ideas rather than competing with "your" and "my" ideas. In the next chapter, we'll help you narrow from your team's favorite ideas to the one you want to courageously try.

Now

You've focused your creativity toward the gap.

You have some great ideas to work with.

You've tapped into each other's creativity.

Take a minute to savor your team's work.

Thank God for the ideas you generated
and the experience you shared with your team.

CHAPTER SIX

Narrow to Your Best Idea: Choosing an Approach that Can Bridge the Gap

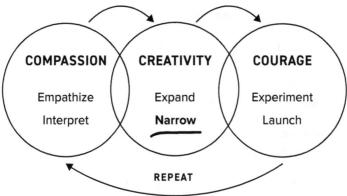

The Sticky Faith Innovation Process

As a leader, you can try to control the outcome or you can learn to guide the process. I chose to guide the process, and it made all the difference.

—Phil, youth leader

You can almost predict the shift.

We watch our Sticky Faith Innovation churches expand their imaginations, and by the end, their workspace is sprawling with colored sticky notes and charts filled with words, ideas, arrows, and pictures. Even those who were nervous about brainstorming have found ways to connect ideas and get excited about the possibilities. The next step—narrowing— turns this process toward focusing your efforts on what your team determines are the best ideas.

And that's when it happens.

Team members begin to realize that their ideas aren't exactly neutral. They're brimming with hopes, dreams, memories, preferences, and even some ego. As teams navigate this narrowing step, we've seen:

- The youth leader go silent because the team wasn't excited about the leader's favorite idea.

- The volunteer leader swear by that one idea that worked for them when they were in high school.

- The senior pastor pretend that everyone has a vote, but it was clear the pastor's "vote" mattered most.

The goal of narrowing is to take your team's best ideas and try to narrow to one idea your team feels will best serve your teenagers in the gap you've identified. The challenge of narrowing is to get there as a whole, intact team! We have discovered that some innovation teams fail to tap into their full creative potential because they couldn't find a way to harmonize their creativity toward one shared idea.

When Irene's team (in Chapter 5) said they "nailed it," they were talking about something much bigger than completing a great project. Irene was telling us that they innovated together, developing an idea they all shared and owned that effectively served their teenagers.

This is why this second *creativity* step is so crucial. It is designed to focus your work and unify your team. Narrowing is all about creatively developing your best ideas further, assessing them, and discerning which idea to experiment with first. We want our best ideas to be owned by more than one enthusiastic person. We want them to be shared. To be *our* idea. Narrowing leads you there.

Creativity turns from expanding to narrowing

The *creativity* move started with expanding your imaginations, which encouraged you to dream and think outside the lines of your current ministry approaches to creatively consider ways of bridging the gap between your teenagers' present realities and all that God desires for them. As you likely guessed or experienced, expanding must eventually wrap up and your team must turn to new, pressing questions like:

What do we choose?

How do we choose?

And, *Who chooses?*

At this stage, these are the right questions to be asking—after your expanding work. This chapter on narrowing helps you focus your team's efforts to make an informed decision on the best way for you to serve your teenagers in the gap where they need you most.

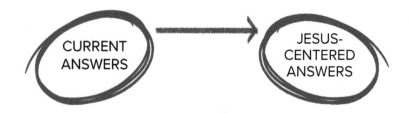

CURRENT ANSWERS → JESUS-CENTERED ANSWERS

Narrowing to focus your team

Like expanding, narrowing requires a process. You and your team have to carefully process your remaining ideas—ensuring you're not rushing through, defaulting to the loudest voice, or simply trying to "keep the peace."

Take your time and don't rush

We've noticed in our Sticky Faith Innovation research that some innovation teams get anxious and push to find a solution as quickly as possible. We get it. Youth ministry can often feel rushed due to ever-present deadlines, parents who want to know what's going to happen next year, or supervisors who are demanding answers. Yet, in narrowing, we ask you to sit with your ideas, talk with your team, and not panic.

Don't rush.

Hang in there.

Your idea and your team will be all the better for it.

Listen to every voice, not just the loud ones

We have also observed that people process together differently. Some are cautious sharers who rarely speak unless asked. Others are verbal processors who speak first, speak long, and speak loud. These types can (often unknowingly) monopolize conversations. When this happens, the team barely has time to hear everyone's perspective, think through their ideas, or come to a unified decision.

Before you narrow, set some ground rules about talking and listening (both are important skills!). Share that you want to respect everyone and give each person equal time to share. Narrowing teaches your team to talk together, work together, and critique together. This step will bring your team closer if your narrowing posture is clear and fair. And if a new program or practice is ever going to move from being an idea to a reality, all voices need to be heard, and everyone truly needs to be on board. After all, no one person will be carrying the innovation all on their own.

Don't "keep the peace"—make the peace

We have also noticed that innovation teams often experience tension when team members get really attached to one idea. When pushed, these team members might shut down or fight back. Passion is great, but it's important to make decisions *together*. When tensions rise, don't decide on one idea just to keep the peace. If the heat is getting too high, it's better to take a short break, returning to the discussion once everyone has had some time to reflect, than it is to choose prematurely to resolve a conflict.

Learn to make space for differences in perspective on your team. No one has the whole picture, so more perspectives are actually better. When tensions rise, recognize this not necessarily as a moment to run or clamp down on the conversation, but to listen more. Help your team wonder together, "What is a team member sharing that I might not otherwise see?" With this posture, we've seen teams have breakthroughs—coming up with better ideas, new solutions, creating deeper unity.

Do more than keep the peace.

Make the peace through healthy dialogue that frees you to work on your ideas, see new perspectives, and serve your students together.

Keep your focus on the gap

We've said it before and it bears repeating: keep your focus on what matters—supporting your teenagers where they need you most. Before you start the process of narrowing, recenter your team on this goal, name the temptations you want to avoid together, accentuate the voices of teenagers on your team, take a deep breath, and then dive in. We'll hang in there with you by providing all the tools needed to focus your ideas so you can decide together which idea to move forward with for the coming season.

Narrowing to focus your ideas

Focusing your team helps you focus your ideas. And to focus your ideas, we encourage you to add detail, evaluate each idea as a team, and share your process with those outside your innovation team to gain input and support.

Narrowing toward greater detail

The narrowing step begins with adding detail to your best ideas. During the expanding step, your team probably came up with some great ideas, but they aren't yet fully formed. To help move toward a decision, add more flesh to the bones of your team's favorite remaining ideas—which takes some imagination.

Imagine for a moment that teenagers were to engage in one of your ideas in exactly the way you hoped they would.

What would they do first?

What would they do next?

What would they do after that?

And what would adult volunteers and other participants be doing at each stage?

To help imagine a program or practice that doesn't yet exist, we suggest a tool that comes from the world of animation called "storyboarding." Before a cartoon is created, animators often create a storyboard of an idea first, creating a sequence of images and corresponding notes to help their team envision a story before it goes to production (see a basic storyboard template in the how-to exercises at the end of the chapter).[26]

Tools like the storyboard can help your team walk out your idea step by step. We have learned from our Sticky Faith Innovation research that teams who did this discovered new questions, anticipated new challenges, and even came up with creative enhancements of their already-great ideas. In the how-to exercises at the end of this chapter, we provide you with a guide to adding detail to your best ideas so your team can better assess them and start narrowing toward a unified decision.

Narrowing to the right idea at the right time: value vs. effort

After detailing out your best ideas, you'll be ready to evaluate them one by one. The best strategy we know for evaluation is to assess each idea's value versus the effort it will take to implement it.

Some ideas might be great, but they may not be achievable.

Weave in Sticky Faith principles

As you imagine the details of your new program or practice, we encourage you to revisit our original Sticky Faith principles to help fill in the details.[27] You can foster teenagers' lasting faith by supporting:

- *intergenerational relationships*
- *family discipleship*
- *space for teenagers to express their doubts*

In our Sticky Faith Innovation research project, we encouraged leaders to consider these principles as they built out their innovative ideas. For example, one youth leader, Damon, and his team learned through their *compassion* work that their students felt pressure and anxiety over their futures. Teenagers shared how the questions adults asked them only exacerbated their stress over school and getting a career. Damon believed that adults in the congregation meant well but their approaches were misguided. As a part of Damon's team's innovation, they came up with the idea of an intergenerational Vocation Fair, modeled off a typical job fair. But instead of advertising job openings, they invited and trained adults in the congregation to sit at "Vocation Booths," ready to share their own career journeys and how God inspired their work. Damon's team prepared the students for the fair by suggesting a few interview questions to help prime conversations, such as, "How is your job a part of God's calling in your life?"

During the event, a student reflected, "I'm learning more about how God led people to particular career paths. It's pretty cool!"

Another student talked with a dentist. While the student didn't have any interest in becoming a dentist, she got excited about how computer software engineering could help the dentist overcome procedural challenges she was facing. The two of them continued to connect beyond the fair.

The impact even went beyond the teenagers. Damon overheard two adults' conversation when one remarked, "We've gone to this church for over 18 years, our kids went to preschool through high school together, and I never knew what you did for a living or how God makes an impact through your career!"

Weaving Sticky Faith principles (like focusing on intergenerational relationships) into your innovative ideas can release new inspiration, making them more relevant and even more effective.

What Sticky Faith principles might strengthen your best ideas?

Other ideas may be easier to implement, but they don't bridge the gap as well.

It's time to chart the way forward using "value vs. effort" as your guide.

VALUE

How do you know if an idea has value? This is where you need to consider how well the idea bridges the gap between your teenagers' current and Jesus-centered answers. It's possible that some remaining ideas are quite innovative, but they don't relate as closely to the current and Jesus-centered answers your team interpreted in the compassion move.

For the sake of illustration, let's imagine that one of the remaining best ideas of Irene's team (from Chapter 5) was to invite teenagers to do speed dating during their midweek youth service (horrible idea, we know). By plugging this idea into the middle "practice/program" blank of their gap sentence, it becomes obvious that this idea really doesn't bridge the gap. Take a look:

Because our teenagers believe, "I have to be perfect or look like it" [current answer]

Teenagers will get to do speed dating at every Wednesday night service [practice/program]

In order that our young people might know, "Even though I am not perfect, God loves me perfectly" [Jesus-centered answer].

It just doesn't sound quite right, does it? The new program or practice in the middle doesn't have any connection to their teenagers' current and Jesus-centered answers. While your remaining ideas won't fit so poorly as this fictional example, filling in the middle blank with each of your new ideas, one-by-one, can help you sense which idea has the most potential to bridge the gap.

EFFORT

After assessing each idea's value, you can then evaluate how much effort it will take to implement it.

How much time, money, or human resources will you need to make this idea a reality?

What might your youth ministry need to give up in order to make time, space, and budget available for this new idea?

Who might need to buy into this idea for it to really take off?

Each of these questions is all about counting the cost. Yet, even if your best idea takes a lot of effort, that doesn't mean you shouldn't do it. In Luke 14:28–30 (MSG), Jesus talks about the cost of discipleship this way:

> *Is there anyone here who, planning to build a new house, doesn't first sit down and figure the cost so you'll know if you can complete it? If you only get the foundation laid and then run out of money, you're going to look pretty foolish. Everyone passing by will poke fun at you: "He started something he couldn't finish."*

Similarly, you need to count the cost of the new ideas you hope to implement to help your teenagers live into more Jesus-centered answers of identity, belonging, and purpose.

Some leaders in our Sticky Faith Innovation research project came up with ideas that cost little, but made a big impact. For example, one church shifted their small group icebreakers in a small but significant way that led to more honest sharing. Rather than doing the traditional "High-Lows," they trained each small group leader to provide these prompts for their students' sharing:

"If you really knew me, you would know ..."

"If I could say anything to God, I would say ..."

This innovation had *high value* (the leader shared that a big cultural shift in the ministry resulted from this change) and *lower effort* to implement.

Other youth leaders came up with ideas that had both *high value* and required *high effort*, like some of the stories we'll share in Chapter 9. Depending on your innovative ideas, they might require raising funds to support families in need, working with leaders from various departments of your church, or building a team to write a whole new curriculum for your small groups.

When you have an idea that can really make a difference, don't let the effort it will take to make it a reality intimidate you. Count the cost, cast a vision, make a plan, and trust the results to God. After charting your best ideas' value vs. effort in the how-to exercises below, chances are you'll know exactly which idea to choose.

Sharing your narrowing

The beauty of the narrowing step is that it encourages your team to work together to decide on your very best ideas. Your team's narrowing journey is as valuable as your ultimate decision. Before fully committing to one idea, it's good to seek input from a broader group of people (like your discernment team) who have a stake in the impact of your innovative approach. This group of people can provide an outside perspective when you help them understand all that has brought your innovative team to this pivotal moment of deciding what to do.

At this stage, one of the most common mistakes youth leaders in our research made was to jump to sharing the details of the new program or practice (about which they were rightly excited) without providing any background as to how their team came up with the idea. How you share your innovative idea requires a careful plan. Luckily, you're already prepared for this! Your gap sentence communicates what you are hoping to do and exactly why you are hoping to do it.

Prepare what you plan to communicate to leaders, parents and guardians, and teenagers before you solicit their input. In doing so, you're bringing them into the process of the innovation at a key moment rather than just asking them to like your idea or give input when they don't have enough context to provide you helpful insight. By communicating well, you'll set them up to offer your innovation team better feedback, help you make a final decision, and be more likely to buy into your new approach in the long run.

From narrowing to choosing

In our cohorts we observed that some churches found choosing one innovative idea challenging because they were excited about many of their possibilities. The how-to exercises at the end of this chapter provide you with important step-by-step instructions to walk out each point that we've described above in order to help your team succeed at narrowing. But before you turn there, remember two things. First, just because you've chosen one idea to innovate doesn't mean you can't try your other ideas later. Save your best ideas. Keep them handy for the future. Narrowing frees you to focus on the one idea your team feels most ready to try right now. Second, rest in the confidence that by this point, of the handful of innovative ideas your team deems the best, you likely can't make a wrong choice. There is more than one way to bridge the gap you seek to address, and by now, you have a number of great ideas that can do just that.

Choose one.

Thank God.

Ask for wisdom to develop it.

And pray for God to turn your creativity toward courage, which is what you need for the final move of Sticky Faith Innovation.

REFLECT

1. When focusing your team to make a decision, which tips from this chapter do you think you'll have to keep most in mind for managing your team dynamics?

REFLECT

2. What excites you about using your imagination
   to detail out your best ideas?

REFLECT

3. What do you feel as you consider sharing your innovation team's best idea with those outside your ministry? Take a moment to process any emotions that come up for you.

HOW-TO EXERCISES FOR NARROWING

These how-to exercises guide you in practically narrowing your options for what new approach to try in your ministry after expanding your options in Chapter 5. This section only makes sense after completing the expanding how-to exercises, so be sure to finish expanding before moving on to these narrowing exercises.

Now that you have expanded your imaginations for what is possible in your ministry, it's time to narrow the options. Narrowing is ultimately about discernment: discerning which ideas have the most potential to form the faith of teenagers in your community, and discerning what God is calling your ministry to in the coming season.

These how-to exercises will help your innovation team:

1. Sketch out some of the best ideas your team came up with and "try them on" to envision how teenagers might experience them.

2. Determine which of your sketched ideas have the most potential to bridge the gap and how much effort they might take to implement.

3. Share your best sketched ideas with your discernment team to get input and invite support.

1) Sketch out your best ideas

Each team member should select their favorite idea they want to develop. If two team members want to collaborate on the same idea, working together in pairs is also a great option.

Individually (or in pairs), work through the Idea Sketch Worksheet below. Schedule a meeting after each innovation team member (or pair) has completed their idea sketch so each idea can be presented to the innovation team.

Idea sketch worksheet

Materials: pen, this worksheet, your favorite idea from the expanding step, and extra scratch paper or journal paper

Instructions:

1. Find a place where you can reflect and write.

2. Review your young people's current answer and Jesus-centered answer.

3. Now reflect, if you were to try this idea:

    a. When would you launch it?

    b. How frequently would it occur, and for how long?

    c. What would it look like? You may want to consider ways in which the practice experiment may incorporate Sticky Faith findings, such as:

    i. Fostering intergenerational relationships

ii. Involving parents and guardians in some way

iii. Creating space for doubt and lament

iv. Ensuring that young people are active participants rather than passive observers

4. Now, on the next page, sketch out what this ministry idea might look like across time. You may wish to draw, write, or storyboard your ideas. Try to get to as much clarity as possible, but do not consider the prep work necessary at this stage (that comes later). This sketch focuses on what engagement in the idea looks like across time. [For example, sketch out what participation looks like across 10 consecutive weeks, thinking about how a teenager would experience it from their perspective.]

Idea sketch meeting

After each team member or pair completes an Idea Sketch, meet together to present your sketches to one another. Team members can then respond to the presented ideas in two ways:

1. "I like ..." (responding to what they really liked about the idea)

2. "I wonder ..." (responding with clarifying questions or additional ideas that build on the ones presented)

The goal is not to decide what to do in this exercise. The goal is to present the best of your ideas, get your teammates' feedback, and note areas that need to be developed further if you ultimately choose to experiment with this idea as a team.

STORYBOARD TEMPLATE

2) Charting value vs. effort

After presenting your idea sketches, it's time to evaluate the ideas by how much effort they will take to implement and by how much potential they have to bridge the gap between teenagers' current and Jesus-centered answers (which is what we mean by "value"). This charting exercise provides you with a tool by which to more objectively evaluate the ideas presented. (And for those of you who may have already landed on one idea, this process can help you discern which aspects of your best idea should be at the core of your new approach, and which aspects should be on the periphery.)

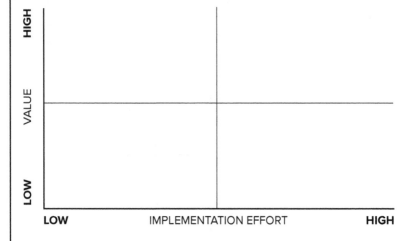

We suggest giving a title to each idea, writing the idea title on a sticky note, and then discussing together as a team where each idea falls on the chart. Any ideas that fall above the middle line for value should move forward to the next round. Ideas below that line may be good ideas, but should not be central to your new approach because your team has deemed that they do not do enough to bridge the gap between teenagers' current and Jesus-centered answers.

Here are the individual sub-steps to complete as an innovation team:

1. Using the Value vs. Effort Chart, plot where each idea falls on the graph.

2. Keep ideas that are above the value line.

3. From the remaining pool of ideas, choose 1–3 ideas to present to your discernment team. Make sure to save the other ideas for later reference.

3) Sharing your top ideas with your discernment team and deciding what to try first

At this stage, it is vital that your innovation team includes a wider circle of trusted leaders to discern the best new ministry approach for the coming season. Your innovation team has been in the trenches of innovation and has done quite a bit of narrowing. Now, your discernment team can bring much-needed perspective before a ministry experiment is officially chosen. To gain the best input from your discernment team, set a time for both teams to share, discuss, and pray together. We suggest setting aside two hours for your time together to share the vision behind your remaining idea(s).

Share

During your discernment team meeting, let the discernment team know what priorities have guided you to your remaining ideas. First, share your gap sentence, which answers:

- What current answer did you discover that seems to drive your young people's quests for identity, belonging, and purpose?

- How do your ideas respond to these formative needs?

- How will this new idea invite young people to follow Jesus' call on their lives?

The discernment team also needs to understand your passion. Why do these ideas excite you? What possibilities do you see? Be sure to provide your discernment team with all they need to know so they can provide valuable insight and guidance.

Discuss

Come prepared with a list of questions you'd like the discernment team to help you think through. Discuss these questions first. Next, provide opportunities for the discernment team to ask questions. You may have thought about answers to some of their questions beforehand and are ready to answer them. For others, you may not be so sure. It's perfectly fine to say you want to discern the answer together. For questions that seem overly specific, explain that none of these ideas are fully planned out. The planning phase comes after deciding which idea to move forward with.

Finally, assure those you share your idea with that you will experiment with the new approach in small form first before you launch anything publicly or make any sweeping changes. You simply want to share this idea with them to get their feedback. (Depending on the size and scope of your innovation, that should hopefully lower their blood pressure!)

Pray

"If any of you is lacking in wisdom, ask God, who gives to all generously and ungrudgingly, and it will be given you." (James 1:5)

The goal of this meeting isn't just to update your team or get your discernment team's insights or approval. The goal is to seek God together. Consider these questions and prompts as you pray and discern a path forward:

1. What is the Holy Spirit saying in light of young people's current answers and the answers you sense God calling them to live into?

2. Which ideas give you hope for your young people, the church, and the surrounding neighborhood?

3. What fears arise as you consider your team's best ideas? Offer these fears to God so you can be guided by faith and not fear.

4. How do these ideas fit into the story of what God is doing in your church and ministry?

Now

You have thoughtfully developed your best ideas.

You have evaluated which ideas have the most value and have counted the cost of how much it will take to implement them.

You have sought the counsel of others and God for what idea to experiment with first.

Well done!

COURAGE

We believe there is success in trying,
In experimenting for learning and growth,
And launching ideas that advocate for young people,
Who are always worth it.

"There is no fear in love.
But perfect love drives out fear..."

—1 John 14:18a

CHAPTER SEVEN

Experiment with Your Best Idea: Testing Your Approach to Make It Better

The Sticky Faith Innovation Process

Experimenting helped us realize that we needed to provide more scaffolding—more clarity—for those participating in our new approach. By testing our idea first, we reduced the risk for everyone and felt more confident about the new program we would eventually launch.

—Shaun, youth leader

I (Caleb) love rock climbing, canyoneering, and cliff jumping. It's great fun, but make no mistake, I'm not a daredevil. Still, even cautious people like me can get caught up in the moment when we're trying to lead others on an exciting excursion.

One time, I took some teenage guys from the youth ministry to go cliff jumping in the mountains. The hike was long and hot, and our adrenaline surged as we reached our destination. I led the way and they followed, flinging boots and shirts off, all of us eager to take the plunge into the cool water below. But right before the leap, something didn't seem right, and I yelled, "Wait! We need to check the depth of the water below first!" The group let out a collective groan and told me to hurry up. I felt bad killing the "extreme" vibe but my guilt evaporated when I discovered that what used to be a 15-foot pool was now only 5 feet deep! We avoided disaster, for sure. (Pro tip: Always check with your leaders and parents before attempting similar excursions!)

Youth leaders' enthusiasm to "go big" too fast with their great ideas can put everything and everyone at risk. It's a temptation for us to talk up our programs, trips, and events by making weighty promises without really testing them first. You've likely witnessed leaders (or yourself!) make a big announcement to teenagers, parents, or the congregation about a ministry initiative that will be game-changingly awesome—only to watch it fail miserably in front of everyone. Big ministry "leaps" are risky. They can erode confidence in your leadership, and most significantly, they can actually hurt people.

But this doesn't mean youth leaders shouldn't dream big or take risks. Treating your innovative idea as an experiment first helps you develop your idea further by testing it in lower risk scenarios. We discovered that leaders in our Sticky Faith

Innovation research project who tested their innovative ideas first established more trust, improved their ideas, and cared well for their communities. One bivocational youth leader shared:

Ministry initiatives have higher stakes than typical secular or business initiatives. I work in marketing for a financial services company, and we try new approaches all the time. We often have an attitude of, "When in doubt, just try it and see what happens—the worst that can happen is we lose a bit of money learning what doesn't work." But when something "doesn't work" in a ministry the result could have a detrimental impact on a community member's spiritual life. Experiments help us try new things with caution out of love for our people. —Haley, youth leader

Remember that success does not rest on launching a big, flashy idea, but in bridging the gap between teenagers' current and Jesus-centered answers to identity, belonging, and purpose.

Perhaps you resonate with Haley's reflections. The great news is that experimenting first made her new ministry initiative even better. Experimenting helps you look before you leap to your full-blown launch. As you build on your work up to this point, you can experiment on a smaller scale in order to refine your new approach, gain momentum, and build your confidence.

Experiment on the wave you're riding

At this point in your Sticky Faith Innovation journey, you have already done a tremendous amount of work to set yourself up for a successful experiment. You have taken the time to compassionately understand your teenagers and interpret their current and Jesus-centered answers to identity, belonging, and purpose, and you've creatively expanded your ministry imaginations and narrowed to your very best idea for the coming season.

Like many leaders from our Sticky Faith Innovation research, you and your team's enthusiasm (and adrenaline!) may be growing and you're eager to launch your project. The wave of the hard, innovative work you've been riding gives you a reason to be excited. But before you launch your innovative idea, there's one important "look" you need to take before you "leap" and that's first trying out your idea as an experiment.

Experiment on the margins (looking before you leap)

Experimenting brings you closer to launching your idea by first testing your program or practice. Our colleague and leadership expert Scott Cormode calls this "experimenting on the margins." It means trying out your innovative idea in a smaller, more controlled environment where there is less risk, more opportunity to receive feedback, and still time to make adjustments.

Experiments need low stakes for implementation

No matter how great your innovative program or practice looks on paper, most youth leaders know that the best-laid plans rarely happen without a hitch—the materials did not work, teenagers needed more time to do an exercise, you forgot to consider the weather, an explanation was confusing, or young people took the idea in a completely different direction than you anticipated. If your first launch is your "big" launch, your one try could make or break the innovation.

In these high-stakes situations, leaders can get distracted from the *purpose* of the new approach. They end up worrying more about whether the experiment "runs smoothly" rather than assessing whether it can accomplish what it sets out to do—bridge the gap. Low-stakes experiments allow for mistakes to be made, schedules to be adjusted, and adaptations to be considered. All these adjustments will refine your innovative new approach to serve your teenagers even better.

Experiments need honest feedback for your own learning

There are some aspects of any plan that are not anticipated until they are experienced. Experiments allow you to gather a small group of teenagers with the express purpose of learning how *they* experience your new ministry approach. Critical to the experiment is creating enough time and space for teenagers to give you their honest feedback. For example, you could ask them:

- What did you like?

- What was confusing?

- How do you think this program or practice might help you?

- What might you do differently?

- If you brought a friend, what would they think?

Do not move forward without teenagers giving you their honest feedback. Let them be your teachers as you learn to make your innovative approach even better.

Experiments need adjustments and course corrections

Without experimenting on the margins first, leaders get tripped up. Sometimes their ideas, mixed with genuine passion (and perhaps a little ego) keep them from being receptive to adjustments. Your small innovation team can become so convinced, so excited, even so tired, that you are unable to hear important feedback. Your team can turn into an echo chamber of similar perspectives that becomes tone-deaf to teenage voices.

Experimenting can reveal both the sturdiest and shakiest parts of the new program or practice. This step gives you the opportunity to listen, learn, and make course corrections to ensure the success of your innovative new approach. In some cases, these may be small tweaks. In others, you may have to adjust your new program's launch date to make bigger changes. Remember that success does not rest on launching a big, flashy idea, but in bridging the gap between teenagers' current and Jesus-centered answers to identity, belonging, and purpose.

Experiment to build trust

By now, you realize that the "innovation" in Sticky Faith Innovation means more than coming up with cool, new ideas. The whole process invites teenagers and adult leaders into a shared process that not only develops better ministry approaches but also cultivates healthier, trusting relationships.

Experiments can grow your relationships with teenagers

Perhaps one of the reasons youth leaders feel that trying something new in ministry is so hard is because teenagers have (rightly) become suspicious of the promises made to them. Young people can be cautious and slow to trust even the most well-meaning adults. Youth leaders from our Sticky Faith Innovation research have told us that low-risk experiments where there is less pressure and more opportunity for young people to give their feedback have nurtured greater trust. As a result, their teenagers have more courage to open up about their real lives, which empowered more successful launches of innovative new approaches in the long run.

Youth leaders in our research caught the importance of experimenting as a crucial step in building relationships with their teenagers. Listen to two of their reflections:

> Launching a new program or practice too fast can actually burn young people out or leave them feeling isolated or like everything is changing. We need to keep learning how to prepare them for change—even positive change.
> —Elizabeth, youth leader

> Experimenting with ideas before launching them helps us—and our teenagers—test the waters of the important changes we're making. Change can be good, but it's always a process of learning and trust.
> —Kurt, youth leader

Leaders like Elizabeth and Kurt remind us all that trust rarely comes from rushing relationships, pumping kids up, or developing the "perfect" event. It typically takes small, experimental steps that build trust and make youth ministries more responsive to our teenagers. Experiments do more than test your innovative idea—they give teenagers a chance to build their relationships with you and others (and they may even become the biggest advocates for your new program or practice!).

Experiments can grow your relationship with church leadership

A consistent theme we heard from youth leaders in our research was that some of the greatest resistance they experienced to innovation came from their church leadership, even after receiving their initial feedback and support during the narrowing step. Pastors or elders would suggest that the timing was no longer right, that the church needed to focus on other priorities, or that their approach contradicted other church commitments given unforeseen changes.

One family pastor confronted a youth pastor, suggesting that their innovation's terminology and theology actually conflicted with the church's already decided upon language and approach. These kinds of encounters can be discouraging. Remember, however, that you have already done careful work empathizing, interpreting, expanding, and narrowing. Those who have not been part of your process may have limited exposure, which brings their reactions of suspicion, fear, even competition.

Trying your idea as an experiment prepares you for these reactions. You can remind your leadership that this is an *experiment*. No, you are not experimenting on young people. Rather, this is a first try with an innovative idea. It is a temporary ministry initiative designed to test the possibilities. No one is trying to make major changes or encroach on another's turf. You are experimenting and learning. We have found that when church leaders see experiments as small attempts rather than a ministry revolution, their concerns dissipate.

Experimenting focuses critique on the experiment and sidesteps unfounded opinions

Even more, the experiment allows you to eventually propose a more substantial initiative to your church leadership with solid data rather than a dreamy idea. Your experiment will allow you to say:

- Here is the problem [current answer, based on your listening]

- This is what we hope for our young people [Jesus-centered answer based on your interpreting]

- Here is what we have tried and learned [experiment]

- And here is what we propose to do [your new program or practice]

Now you are bringing a solid argument with actual data to the leadership table. Those church leaders who have different views of teenagers, what they need, or what the youth ministry ought to do about it now need to support their views just like you have. Framing your idea as an experiment levels the playing field to discuss the merits of your innovative idea rather than arguing over opinions.

In our experience, this may be exactly what church leaders need from you. In 99 percent of cases, their resistance does not come from hoping you fail, but because they really want you to succeed (deep down they care about young people, too!). The Sticky Faith Innovation process gives your church leaders clarity, evidence, and confidence in your thinking and planning.

Remember the family pastor that had "concerns" about the youth pastor's innovative new approach? The youth leader's careful explanation of the goals of the new approach, skillful testing on the margins, and ongoing conversations helped the family pastor realize that their new ministry approach would elevate the church priorities, not compete with them. In the end, she became the youth worker's biggest advocate.

We think this is every youth leader's dream. It's a dream this leader prayed for and worked hard to realize.

Experiment toward the vision (innovating in the right direction)

Your innovative new approach is not the end in itself. Thus, your ultimate goal must be more than "hoping your experiment goes well." Experimenting positions you for much more.

Experiments give your team room to grow

Sometimes youth ministry teams spend so much effort on rolling out programs that people are left in the dust. Volunteer leaders get burned out, discouraged, or even feel used by their leaders. Here's your chance to not only evaluate your experiment but also check in with your innovation team. Consider asking these non-programmatic questions:

- What did you learn through our experiment about yourself and about our teenagers?

- What kinds of emotions did you feel throughout the experiment? What might they be telling you?

- Where might God be encouraging you and us to grow?

Your fellow youth leaders want to do more than keep the youth ministry machine going. They want to grow, change, and experience God in their lives. Give them permission to consider their own brushes with the holy.

Experiments test whether your new approach can bridge the gap

Notice how experimenting works. It shifts the goal from "Did the project go well?" to "Did this new approach address the gap we're trying to bridge?" Remember, if innovation is about helping your teenagers live into Jesus-centered answers, experimenting allows you to listen to them to hear how your work is truly helping them. Now you're spending more time trying to improve the way your youth ministry bridges the gap rather than trying to come up with catchy ways to market toward their attention.

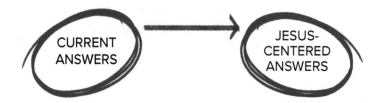

You're looking before you leap.

Showing up where teenagers need you most.

With eyes wide open.

REFLECT

1. The challenge of this step is actually trying out your innovative idea. What worries come up for you? Take a minute to jot them down. Ask God for courage.

REFLECT

2. Your experiment will likely have some bright spots and some misses.

   a. How well do you take feedback, and are people willing to give it to you?

   b. Where might you need to grow in receiving constructive feedback?

REFLECT

3. Who on your innovation team needs encouragement and support? Who needs clarity? Who needs to refocus on the purpose of the new ministry approach? Jot down your thoughts. Lead your team, and help them grow.

HOW-TO EXERCISES FOR EXPERIMENTING

Experimenting gives you the opportunity to test your innovative idea on the margins so you can learn from trying and adjust your idea to make it better for your actual launch (Chapter 8).

These how-to exercises will help you and your team:

1. Set up your experiment to simulate and experience your innovative approach.

2. Invite honest and helpful feedback that will make your innovative approach even better.

3. Grow your courage to eventually launch your innovative approach to address the gap.

Setting up your experiment

The best way to set up your experiment is by treating it as though you were going "live" with your innovation. Treat it with equal care, planning, scheduling, and hopefulness. The more "real" you make your experiment, the better feedback you will get. With this in mind, be sure to answer the following questions as you set it up.

- Who will participate in the experiment? (When you talk about it with others, you may want to call it a "test run" of a new approach, as the word "experiment" out of context can sound strange to teenagers and parents. To quote one youth leader, "Parents don't want you to experiment with their kids, so I had to frame what we are doing in terms of customization for these kids out of empathy, rather than 'innovation.'")

- Limit the number of participants to the minimum number necessary to effectively test your new program or practice. This will ensure you do not have too few but also not so many that you cannot get personal feedback from all those participating.

- Consider inviting people from diverse backgrounds (based on age, gender, ethnicity, and connection with the youth ministry) so that you get a range of perspectives.

- When you ask teenagers, be very clear on why you've invited them and that you are interested in their honest input. Teenagers need clarity on what you are asking them to do.

• When—on what date and at what time—will we attempt the experiment?

- Schedule your experiment far enough in advance so people can plan to attend. Be sure to communicate the date and your expectations for participating.

- Additionally, be sure to schedule enough time to debrief the experience at the end.

- How will we test our program or practice to ensure that it works?

  – Will you test the whole innovation at once or in different portions?

  – What is at the heart of your new approach? At a minimum, be sure to test out what is central to your new program or practice.

- How will we solicit feedback?

  – Ask questions that help teenagers, parents and guardians, and any others involved share how they felt about the experiment experience. Remember that people process differently. You may want to offer some discussion, writing, individual, and group feedback options. Try these questions for starters:

    › What did you like?

    › What was confusing?

    › How do you think this program or practice might help you?

    › What might you do differently?

    › If you brought a friend, what would they think? (for teenagers)

    › What was the impact on your family schedule or other church programming? (for adults)

  – As soon as possible, compile your feedback. Create a document that captures all the input, and then work on a summary page that identifies the most salient information that you believe you must pay attention to as a team.

  – What outstanding questions does your innovation team have?

Evaluating your experiment

Based on your summary document of feedback from your teenagers, adults, and your own team, you can now evaluate your experiment. This will likely include "how the experiment went," but may also raise your awareness about where your teaching or explanation must be clearer or your activities were too long or short, too complicated, or just didn't work. Here are some prompts for your evaluation.

People

- Do we have the right people in the right roles?

- Are we, as leaders, all on the same page? What do we need to do to resolve confusion or differences?

- What further training might we need to offer leaders?

Communication

- Did we set up and communicate the experiment well to those participating?

- Were participants clear on what they were doing? What could be clearer? What could be made simpler?

Logistics

- How did the experiment flow logistically?

- How did our planned schedule compare to the actual experiment?

- Did we provide the right timing, space, and materials?

  - What took too long?

  - What seemed rushed, or where did people need more time?

   – Did we have the right materials?

   – What would we change, add, remove?

Experience

- What did teenagers find exciting, encouraging, meaningful, or helpful?

- Where did they get stuck, confused, frustrated, or bored?

- What stories or comments did the experience raise?

Adjusting your experiment

Based on your feedback summary, describe the elements that worked really well and those that need adjustments. Based on the kind of feedback you get, you may not only need to adjust your innovation, you may need to recalibrate your timeline if major changes are needed. In some cases, you may want to listen to teenagers more, refine your interpreting work, expand your options once more, or run another experiment to test any adjustments you've made. The innovation process isn't always linear, because it involves a lot of learning—which is the very purpose of experimenting on the margins!

- What common feedback themes emerged?

- Of these themes, which top three elements should we ensure we keep?

- Of these themes, which top three elements do we need to improve or change?

- List all the adjustments you will make.

Now

You've tested your innovative idea.

You've gained more insight by soliciting feedback from those you aim to serve.

And your courage is growing.

Let's get ready to launch...

CHAPTER EIGHT

Launch Your Innovative Approach: Stepping Out with Faith and Courage

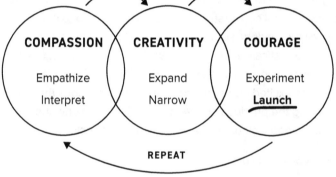

The Sticky Faith Innovation Process

COMPASSION

Empathize

Interpret

CREATIVITY

Expand

Narrow

COURAGE

Experiment

Launch

REPEAT

After we introduced our innovative practice for the first time, one of my students told me that it was the most spiritually impactful youth ministry gathering she had experienced in a very long time.

—Jill, youth leader

I (Steve) was hosting my first youth leader retreat as a new pastor of a faith community. It was the first night of the event and I was minutes away from making my first, big "vision message" to our youth leader staff and volunteers. The stakes felt really high. These are the moments when first impressions can set you on a great trajectory or set you back. I needed to nail it.

Just before I was to go on, I ran to the restroom (pre-speaking jitters). As I was drying my hands, one of our volunteer youth leaders entered. Restrooms feel like elevators—the space is way too small to ignore those sharing it yet way too awkward for meaningful conversation. Already psyched up to connect with all the leaders, I decided to bridge the awkward moment by enthusiastically introducing myself. He greeted me, too. We had a nice, short conversation, and I kept trying to get a sense if he was excited about the new pastor or suspicious that I was replacing the previous one. As I left the restroom, he shouted to me, "Good luck out there. Hope you don't suck."

Hope you don't suck.

That's what every leader wants to hear when you feel like you're taking a risk and the stakes are high.

Perhaps you can relate to those big ministry moments when you're putting it all on the line. You've felt the weight of your decisions where success or failure hung in the balance. Like you, the leaders in our innovation cohorts eventually arrived at this tipping point. The empathizing, interpreting, expanding, narrowing, and experimenting work they did was fun, hard work, and helpful, but then they recognized they had to deliver.

Put it on the line.

Go for it.

Launch: go for it!

Launching an innovative idea can feel scary, and the anxiety can rob leaders of their confidence and follow-through. This is the moment you step out and take a risk for your teenagers, putting your own reputation on the line. It's terrifying and, honestly, no one wants to suck. Don't worry. The Sticky Faith Innovation process has you covered. First, the innovation process has increased your chances for success. We're talking about more than wishful thinking—you've taken thoughtful steps toward your young people's greatest needs.

Second, remember that it's better to try and fail than not to try. Fear has a way of telling us to return to our old ways, doubt our work, or worry about the results. Launching is truly a step of faith, and we'll only grow when we try.

Let this sink in—*trying* is a win!

Jesus seemed to embrace this outlook. He told his disciples to "ask," "seek," "knock" (Luke 11:9). In other words, "Go for it." That's trying. That's faith. James caught it, writing, "You don't have because you don't ask God" (James 4:2). The places where faith flourishes are where Jesus-followers try.

Perhaps we all need this reminder. Youth ministry can easily default to managing risk rather than taking risks. Perhaps what young people need from their youth leaders is to witness your own risk-taking and your willingness to thoughtfully "go for it," in Jesus' name.

Launching well

Launching your new program or practice is the moment when you need your courage the most—to make your new idea a reality in hopes of bridging the gap between teenagers' current answers and the answers God desires for them. Now is the time to lean in, take courage, and remember three principles to help guide you as you launch your new program or practice: train before you launch, make it simple, and invite personally.

Train leaders, change leaders

Many of the leaders in our Sticky Faith Innovation research project came up with exciting and creative ideas, but not every new program or practice had the same degree of impact. We noticed that one of the key differences was in the way the ministry teams trained (or didn't train) their adult volunteers. Those whose innovations had less of an impact often mistook orientation for training. What's the difference?

Orientation is when you introduce your volunteers to the basic details of the new program or practice. These are the details you might find on a Frequently Asked Questions sheet (we'll suggest you create one of these in the how-to exercises at the end of this chapter), answering the *who, what, where, when, and why* of the new approach. While leaders gain a general sense of the approach, orientations don't go far enough to invite them into the process. Here's where training comes in.

Training is when you equip your leadership team with all they need to know and experience in order to invest in your innovative launch. Without training, volunteer leaders tend to default to their typical youth ministry roles, whether that's "keeping the kids in line," blending in with them, or sitting on the sidelines. Volunteer leaders often wonder, "Where am I supposed to be right now, and what am I supposed to do?" Training answers this question and provides clear guidance on their roles in accomplishing your new approach's goal of discipling teenagers.

At one church, Braven realized that the success of his

team's innovative new approach rested on training. Through their listening, the team had learned that the many at-risk teenagers who attend their church were coming to escape and ignore their pain rather than work through it. Yet Braven and his team wanted the youth group to be more than a fun escape from reality. They realized they needed to help teenagers process their pain and find God in the midst of it. While Braven's leaders were truly amazing, he was determined not to assume they would know what to do to make this new vision a reality. He set out to train his leadership team so they would have all the skills and knowledge they needed for the new approach. Let's break down exactly what Braven did.

First, Braven recruited several adult leaders who had prior experience working with at-risk teenagers and then paired them with existing adult volunteers. Next, they all learned more together about asset-based youth work, suicide prevention, lament, and how to build trust with at-risk youth through consistency and support. After this training and several months into their new approach, Braven reflected, "Training adult leaders was really at the core of this project. Without a team of well-trained, well-equipped adult leaders, there's no way we would be able to serve some of these at-risk students."

After equipping adults, the youth ministry was able to offer at-risk teenagers increased support, meeting many of their basic needs by providing clothing, temporary housing, school supplies, and meals. In receiving this care and participating in other aspects of the innovation, several students opened up about past and present experiences of abuse. Because of the training they had received, the volunteers were able to step into these significant spaces of instability and offer the support and guidance these teenagers needed. Instead of avoiding challenges like these, the team was trained to embrace them—*and* they knew when to refer teenagers to professional mental health resources. Teenagers were supported, and adults grew along with them.

The launch of your new approach will be more successful when you not only train your leaders to implement it, but also prepare them for their own transformation. Check out the how-to exercises at the end of this chapter for practical instructions to train your team to be fully prepared for the new program or practice.

Keep it simple: create a mantra

By this point in your Sticky Faith Innovation journey, the "why" behind your new approach to ministry is clear—you want to help bridge the gap between your teenagers' current and Jesus-centered answers, to help them develop a faith that lasts. Yet what might be obvious to you may not be clear to others who haven't been through the same innovation process with you. When you "go public" with your new approach, it's important that you get to the heart behind your innovation as simply as possible. People remember simple.

We discovered that youth leaders in our research who created a phrase or mantra for their new approach were more easily able to remember and share their innovative initiative with others. More people knew about it, and more people got excited about it.

For example, one team innovated a new intergenerational midweek service and came up with the mantra, "Make space for what matters most." The team wanted to communicate how important developing intergenerational relationships is and motivate teenagers and adults to participate with them. Another church reimagined how to incorporate reflective practices like journaling into their youth gatherings to prepare teenagers to share their testimonies with one another. Their mantra was, "Know God. Know self. Share both." These six words powerfully communicated the heart of their innovation. And another innovation team wanted to help their teenagers know they had worth outside of what they produced by practicing restful Sabbaths together. Their mantra was simple: "Be."

As you look to launch your new program or practice, what mantra simply and memorably communicates the heart of your new approach? Look to the how-to exercises to help you and your team come up with a mantra that your students can remember and repeat.

Tell one, tell all

Launching also requires that you let people know that your new program or practice is happening! The instinct is often to get the word out through different channels, like social media, church announcements, and mailers. Communication strategies like these are important so people become aware of what's going on. Yet young people (and all people) don't just want to know something is happening. They also want to know you personally want them there. Make personal invitations more than an afterthought. Make them a priority.

One church in our Sticky Faith Innovation research project took this idea of personal invitation quite seriously and launched a student-led welcome team. The welcome team greeted everyone who came, looked for those who were alone to start conversations, and invited them to participate in various activities. This student-led team eventually grew to a third of the entire youth group and helped make their innovation a success.

As you prepare to launch, start to consider not only what you're going to do but who you are personally going to invite.

Look to the how-to exercises for help with putting an invitee list together with your team and assigning whom each team member will invite. Personal invitations can truly make or break the launch of your new approach!

Launching now

In one of my coaching calls with a youth leader named Tara, I (Caleb) remember how nervous she was just before the launch of their new program. Tara asked, "But what if it doesn't work?" Tara's team had come up with one of those kinds of ideas that could really only work if the Spirit of God showed up, moved people's hearts, and created relationships that didn't exist before. No matter how well she and her team had prepared, it could still be a flop. It was at this moment that I realized that Tara and her team were taking the right kind of risks. They had done their homework, planned, and prepared extremely well—but in the end, their idea would only work if God was in it. They were really going for it. That's what courage looks like.

As youth leaders, we are called by God to take courageous and faithful risks that rely on God to come through and do what only God can do. In response to Tara's question, I answered, "You've led so well and have done everything you needed to prepare for this moment. And now, we just need to pray." Then I prayed this prayer over her, which we now extend to each of you:

Dear God, thank you for this faithful leader and this leader's incredible team. Thank you for guiding them to this moment. We humbly come before you, Lord, and ask that you would do what only you can do. They have prepared the way, and now we simply ask that you would come. Have your way, O God."

Take courage, friends. You're just about ready to launch. To go for it. And perhaps, like Tara and the three leaders whose stories we share in the next chapter, you'll see your innovative idea as even more than a program or practice. It's a true step of faith for you all.

REFLECT

1. When you think about "going for it," what feelings come up for you? Take a moment to journal and process through these emotions.

REFLECT

2. Of the three essential launch tips mentioned in this chapter, which comes the most naturally to you and your team, and which seems like it'll take the most effort or learning?

REFLECT

3. In what areas do you feel you'll especially need to rely on God as you launch your new program or practice? Pause and pray, asking God to do what only God can do.

HOW-TO EXERCISES FOR LAUNCHING

You've leveraged your compassion and creativity through a careful process that gives you reason to have courage to take your innovative approach to the gap where your teenagers need you most.

These how-to exercises set you up to accomplish the following:

1. Train (or retrain) your team with what they need to know and do to contribute to a successful launch.

2. Create a mantra your leaders can practice and share with others and that teenagers can remember.

3. Make a list of the teenagers, adults, parents, or leaders you'd personally like to invite to participate.

4. Pray with confidence that God will bring fruit to your efforts.

Train your team

Before you launch your new program or practice, you need to train your volunteer leaders so they know where they are supposed to be and what they are supposed to do at various stages of your new ministry approach.

Orientation

To prepare your team well, begin with an orientation. You might consider creating a list of Frequently Asked Questions (FAQ). The process of developing an FAQ helps you ensure you have covered all your bases, and it serves as a helpful resource not only for your volunteer team, but for your teenagers, parents, and the congregation as a whole. (It also acts as a bit of proof for your leadership that you've done your homework!)

We encourage you to answer in some form:

1. What is this new program or practice? Summarize it briefly.

2. Why are we doing this program or practice? Explain how the program or practice bridges the gap between your current and Jesus-centered answers. You may want to share your mantra, as well.

3. When and where will this program or practice take place? Share the start date, meeting times, duration, and location.

4. Who should participate? Explain who you hope will participate and who is at the heart of your new program or practice (likely young people).

5. Additionally, answer any other questions you anticipate parents, leaders, and teenagers may ask.

Training

In addition to an orientation, you should provide more robust training. To train well, consider:

1. Based on our experimenting with this new approach in the previous courage step, where did our innovation team and other leaders feel most uncertain?

2. What do our volunteer leaders need to know and experience before they can lead teenagers through the new program or practice? How will we provide this knowledge and experiential learning?

3. Who might we recruit to provide additional training for our team and/or to join our team?

4. When and over what period of time will we provide training? Consider whether training should overlap with the launch of your new approach, or if it should all take place before the launch.

Make your mantra

As a team, meet together to brainstorm mantras that communicate the heart of your new program or practice. Mantras should be:

1. Simple
2. Memorable
3. Repeatable

Simple: Try to keep your mantra to seven words or less.

Memorable and Repeatable: Consider using alliteration (i.e., several words in the phrase start with the same letter), assonance (i.e., several words have the same vowel sound), or rhyme to give your mantra flow and to make it catchier.

Once your team lands on a mantra you all like, incorporate this mantra into all your communication about your new ministry approach.

Invite participation

As an innovation team, make a list of who each team member will personally invite to participate in the new approach and set a deadline by which personal invitations should be made.

	Leader	Person to be Invited
1.		
2.		
3.		
4.		
5.		
6.		
7.		
8.		
9.		
10.		

Invitation Deadline: _____

Trust God for the results

Finally, trust God for the results. After doing all the work you've done, it's important to remember that your team can plant and water, but only God can make it grow (see 1 Cor. 3:6). You have done faithful work. Entrust the results to God.

A pre-launch team prayer:

God, we have come so far, and yet, up to this point, it has all been preparation. We ask, Lord, that you would do what only you can do. We pray that through the work of our hands and your Spirit, teenagers would find their identity, belonging, and purpose in you. Amen.

Now

You can be encouraged by your faithful work.

You've trusted your team and together, you're trusting God...

To guide you to stand in the gap with your teenagers,

With people cheering you on.

Have courage!

VISION

STICKY FAITH **INNOVATION**

It begins when you realize the world needs more of your compassion, creativity, and courage.

It celebrates every time you advocate for one more young person.

"Very truly I tell you, whoever believes in me will do the works I have been doing, and they will do even greater things than these, because I am going to the Father."

—John 14:12

CHAPTER NINE

Sticky Faith Innovation Stories: Everyday Churches that Inspire Compassion, Creativity, and Courage

Sticky Faith Innovation is more than theory—it's led to amazing stories of youth leaders like you who have channeled their compassion, creativity, and courage to support their teenagers where they need them most. In this chapter, we share some of the stories we've had the privilege of watching unfold. These stories serve as beautiful, inspirational examples of what your compassion, creativity, and courage can do for young people, your church, and you. May their innovative new approaches inspire your own innovative work!

Church story profiles

You might think these snapshots come from big churches with mega-budgets. They don't. In fact, the first church has less than 200 people, the second less than 300, and the last less than 400. Each church hails from a different part of the country, and they each hold a rich denominational tradition that has shaped their identity and, at times, brought about resistance to change. Our point is this: these churches reflect the vast majority of churches in the United States—faithful churches with limited budgets, congregational worries, committed youth leaders, and amazing young people. Whether your church is big or small, Sticky Faith Innovation can help you meet your teenagers where they need you most.

A Story of Compassion – City Church

"This is the stupidest thing I've ever heard of. I'm never going to do this." Not exactly the words you want to hear from a teenager when you try something for the first time in your youth ministry.

While working on their compassion move, Connor's innovation team had listened to their teenagers, and their students were honest: they felt alone, unloved, and didn't think they could have a purpose outside of finding an hourly job at some point in the distant future. It was actually hard for Connor's team to hear their pain and disillusionment. Yet they hung in there and kept listening.

Through prayer and discernment over what they sensed Jesus would want to say to their teenagers, the team came up with this: "You are fully known and still loved." To bridge the gap between their teenagers' current and Jesus-centered answers, they decided to innovate around the practice of lament for their youth group. They longed for their young people to discover that God cares about what they've been through, is with them in their pain, and isn't intimidated by their anger or grief.

Connor's team was excited to try their new practice with their teenagers, but 16-year-old José just wasn't having it.

"This is stupid. Why am I going to complain to God about all the sh*t that's happened in my life? He doesn't care."

Connor and his team had developed creative ways for their teenagers to lament to God through yoga, painting, and writing songs, poems, and spoken words, but they started second-guessing themselves after José's reaction. Yet, thankfully, the other teenagers in the group seemed cautiously open and willing to give it a try.

City Church's gap sentence:

Because our teenagers believe, *"I am so alone, I don't feel anymore"* [current answer]

We will innovate *a way for our teenagers to learn, experience, practice, and live into the Christian practice of lament, allowing them to feel again and be honest with Jesus in the context of their faith community* [practice/program]

In order that our young people might know, *"Even though I am not perfect, God sees me as perfectly loved"* [Jesus-centered answer].

Week after week, the youth group gathered and Connor invited his students to lament. The more opportunities the teenagers had, the more honest they became with God and each other. The pain they slowly started to reveal was extraordinary and heartbreaking. One week, a teenager broke down and sobbed, "They keep making fun of me because I smell. But we don't have any running water at home." This lament prompted Connor to visit the girl's home the next day. He was shocked by what he found: the gas and water had been cut off, and the family was struggling to put food on the table.

Three months later, what started as a small experiment practicing lament in the youth group led to the church opening shower and laundry facilities, budget management classes, and family dinner nights during the Wednesday night youth group meeting. The entire congregation rallied around the families in their church and community who were facing enormous need.

Today, as a result of their innovative journey, Connor's youth group has become a nonprofit that partners with the city to bring care to families in the community who are facing food insecurity and poverty.

When Connor told us about their innovation and all that it led to, we were dumbfounded. It surpassed our wildest expectations. He shared with us,

> *If we hadn't reimagined lament for our community, our youth group would have never made the impact it is having today. But I'll be honest, in my 25 years of being a youth leader, I've never been so exhausted. Yet I've also never been so sure that I'm doing what God has called me to do. Lament is helping our whole church grieve the "good old days" from fifty years ago to meet families' needs today, helping them turn toward the future. Oh, and you know what? José is now the first person to share his laments each week, and he's encouraging teenagers new to our ministry to do the same.*

Perhaps you noticed that what drove Connor's youth group to begin these new initiatives started with opening their hearts toward each other and to God. Their compassion led to creative expressions of lament; lamenting opened up their teenagers' hearts; and their teenagers' vulnerability made way for the church to care for their families' greatest needs.

A Story of Creativity – New Atlantic Church

Jordan's innovation team wanted their young people to know that their gifts and passions matter to God and can make a lasting impact in their church and community. But when they started innovating, they began regretting not having any teenagers on their team. They realized they had missed something critical, and as a result got frustrated with themselves. Their creative juices stopped flowing.

New Atlantic Church's gap sentence:

Because our teenagers believe, *"I'm stuck in a purpose that has been chosen for me"* [current answer]

We will innovate *a way for our teenagers to use their gifts and passions to serve God and others* [practice/program]

In order that our young people might know, *"My gifts and passions matter to God, and I can make a lasting impact in my church and community"* [Jesus-centered answer].

But then Veronica (a new volunteer and member of the innovation team) wondered out loud, "What if we taught our teenagers to innovate?" The team fell silent. "What if we taught our students to innovate, and we unleashed *their* creativity? That might even be better than if we had one or two teenagers on our team." At that moment, the team knew that's exactly what they needed to do.

Three months later, after discussing the idea with their teenagers, Jordan and his team launched their first-ever summer apprenticeship program, in which each teenage apprentice walked through the Sticky Faith Innovation process—empathizing with the people they hoped to serve, creatively coming up with ideas to meet their needs, and then putting them into action. Students empathized with anyone from older adults in the church to children to those leading the social media department. Jordan's team fueled young people's creativity and passion, and the results were phenomenal.

One teenager, Cynthia, wanted to focus on elderly care ministry. When Jordan asked her what led her to that emphasis, she confessed, "To be honest, I'm kind of afraid of old people. But I want to overcome that fear." By the end of the apprenticeship, Cynthia and her team of teenagers had successfully connected the entire congregation to the oldest among them through interactive prayer cards.

When Jordan met with Cynthia to debrief her apprenticeship experience, he asked her if she still felt nervous around elderly people in the church. She replied, "Actually, before doing this apprenticeship, I already knew I wanted to be a nurse. Now, I want to specialize in geriatrics!" Another apprentice redesigned a meeting room into a children's theater, another established a rideshare program to help those without transportation get to church, while others improved the church's social media presence, worked on offering fair trade coffee at the church, and set up live streaming for weekend services. Each teenager was able to focus on an area that mattered to them personally, and saw how their gifts and passions made a difference in the church.

It was so rewarding for us at FYI to hear how Jordan's team made the Sticky Faith Innovation process come alive for their teenagers, and how it turned into a transformative experience for their young people and the whole church. When we followed up with Jordan to hear more about his experiment, he shared,

> It went so well, and I learned so much along the way. One of the biggest lessons I learned was about working with leaders in different areas of the church. Looking back, when we presented the idea to leadership, we forgot to include the importance of the listening and empathy exercises teenagers would do at the beginning and that

apprentices would be paired with the leaders for guidance and mentoring. As a result, some leaders thought the apprentices were going to take over their ministries. We had to do a lot of work to win back their trust. But, in the end, we did. And it was so amazing to see how our apprentices experienced their passions and gifts being used in the church beyond what they thought possible.

New Atlantic Church's youth ministry may have also made another important discovery—that Sticky Faith Innovation might not just unleash your creativity. It might even unleash the creativity of your teenagers as well! That's something we at FYI get excited about.

A Story of Courage – Heartland Church

Should we really try to involve the whole congregation? It'd be so much easier if we didn't.

Heartland Church's innovation team was nearing the end of the narrowing step in the Sticky Faith Innovation process, and they reached a fork in the road:

Lane 1: They could keep the idea focused on their youth ministry.

Lane 2: They could try to involve the whole church.

On one hand, focusing on their youth ministry would allow them to still impact their teenagers and (quite honestly) save them from the logistics of working with the whole church. On the other hand, including the whole congregation had the potential of encouraging intergenerational dialogue, but teenagers might get lost in the process.

This would be an easy decision: *Lane 1, please!*

But then Jen chimed in, "But if we involve the whole church, teenagers would actually get to know adults in the church who would never set a foot in the youth room. And if parents and teenagers were going through the same process, we might actually help whole families grow closer to God and each other. Wouldn't that be worth it?"

Jen's question hung in the air.

Yes, it would be. But there was no telling if all the needed church leaders would get on board, let alone like the idea. Including the whole congregation would make the idea so much more valuable in helping teenagers develop lasting faith (through creating intergenerational relationships and involving parents),[28] but it would also take so much more effort to implement it.

In the end, the team decided, "Let's go for it. Worst-case scenario, leadership says 'no' and we keep it to the youth group. Best-case scenario, this can make a huge impact on not only our teenagers, but our entire church."

Six months later, Jen and her team sat listening to testimony after testimony of people ages 11 to 91 sharing how God was at work in their lives. In a congregation that rarely shared personal stories, the words they heard coming out of the mouths of young and old alike were truly miraculous. Tears ran down their cheeks as a middle-aged man from the congregation shared the message he had believed for so much of his life—that he was a mistake, being the child of an affair. But then he declared to the congregation, "But that message can't overturn the truth of Genesis 1—God made me good."

Their hearts swelled as a teenager shared her story of feeling alone and not wanting to attend youth group anymore, but how she ultimately found friendship through listening to the stories of other teenagers and learning to share her own in her storytelling small group.

Their smiles grew as a parent expressed how she never would have stood on stage to share her story with the whole church had she not been able to practice telling it in the storytelling workshop.

Somehow, all of their innovation team's work came to fruition. The crazy idea Nathaniel had to create a storytelling booth where people could privately video-record their stories in the foyer actually worked. People they never expected to try it, including 91-year-old Mary, stepped inside and recorded their stories. And then, each week the senior pastor included snippets from people's testimonies in his Sunday sermons.

James's idea to bring in a storytelling expert to host a workshop gave those who shared their stories at the storytelling night confidence to speak in front of the whole congregation. And Sara's idea to gather a diverse team from across different areas of the church to develop age-based storytelling small group curricula for teenagers, parents, and adults created a unity in the church they had never experienced before.

Reflecting back on these experiences, Jen shared this note with our FYI team,

> *I learned some very important lessons in our Sticky Faith Innovation journey, but the biggest of all was this: You can't do big things unless you dream big things. We would have never seen all the transformation in people's lives and in the life of our church had we not been willing to come up with crazy ideas and risk asking the whole church to be a part of them. We would have never had the level of impact we did if we kept it to the youth group alone.*

At important moments along the way, Jen and her team accessed their courage to develop more lasting faith in their teenagers, and in the lives of the hundreds of other adults who participated in their innovative ideas with them. Sometimes going the courageous route means realizing that your choice between "Lane 1" and "Lane 2" is a false choice, and God is asking you to move into "Lane 3," which incorporates all lanes for a bigger, more profound vision.

You can't do big things unless you dream big things.
—Jen, youth leader

Now, it's your turn

What inspires us about these stories is that each leader compassionately empathized with their young people, creatively expanded their imaginations for what was possible, and courageously took steps to make their homegrown ideas a reality. Each story is unique—as unique as their young people. And so are yours.

REFLECT

1. Sometimes, small innovations lead to bigger change down the road. What about Connor's team's innovation inspires or encourages you?

REFLECT

2. Jordan's team directly involved teenagers in innovation. How might you include more teenagers in your future innovative efforts?

REFLECT

3. Jen learned in her Sticky Faith Innovation journey, "You can't do big things unless you dream big things." What keeps you from dreaming big? What might help you take some thoughtful risks to see young people's lives and the life of the church transformed?

CHAPTER TEN

Sticky Faith Innovation Vision: A Renewed View for Youth Ministry

The Sticky Faith Innovation process CHANGED the way our team ministered to young people. It gave us permission to dream—and dream big—and the resources to help us implement and achieve those dreams, not just in our youth ministry but for our church as a whole.

—Jen, youth leader

The original Sticky Faith research discoveries we made a decade ago set the Fuller Youth Institute on a trajectory that amplified our convictions: youth ministries do best when they advocate for teenagers together with their congregations and parents. Since then, we have conducted more research and created more resources to equip church leaders, parents, stepparents, grandparents, and guardians in multiple and diverse settings to be the best advocates for teenagers and emerging adults.

FYI RESOURCES FOR YOU

Kara Powell, Jake Mulder, and Brad Griffin,
Growing Young: Six Essential Strategies to Help Young People Discover and Love Your Church, (Grand Rapids: Baker Books, 2016)

Kara Powell and Steven Argue,
Growing With: Every Parent's Guide to Helping Teenagers and Young Adults Thrive in Their Faith, Family, and Future, (Grand Rapids: Baker Books 2019)

Fuller Youth Institute, *Multicultural Youth Ministry [multiple resources]*, 2020, fulleryouthinstitute.org/multicultural

Fuller Youth Institute, *The FYI on Youth Ministry Podcast*. Season 2 is focused on Sticky Faith Innovation. Subscribe on iTunes or listen at fulleryouthinstitute.org/podcast

Everyone plays a role in supporting young people. Yet, as our colleague Kara Powell often says, "If you want to starve a horse, tell two people to feed it." In other words, asking two people to feed a horse risks that each person will assume the other is handling it, and the horse starves. We face the same risk in youth ministry. If we assume everyone is responsible for helping teenagers' faith stick, no one may end up doing it—and teenagers spiritually starve.

That's why we wrote this book specifically to you, youth leader. Every adult can play an important role in a teenager's life; yet in Sticky Faith Innovation, we have championed your role. Young people need *your* compassion, creativity, and courage to advocate for them. The church needs you to lead the way in supporting teenagers' lasting faith. And we know you can. In this chapter, we cast a vision for expanding the impact Sticky Faith Innovation can have on teenagers, youth ministry, and the entire congregation—led by you and your team.

Leading a youth ministry that inspires compassion, creativity, and courage

The Sticky Faith Innovation process is a repeatable cycle that can keep calling you to deepen your compassion, creativity, and courage. After you have launched one new initiative, you can return to this process again to discern your ministry's next faithful step. With repeated attempts, you and your team will grow in your innovative capacities, making you more responsive to your teenagers today and tomorrow. This innovative process can transform the way you lead your team, using it to cultivate grassroots ideas, focus your priorities, and include others.

Cultivate grassroots ideas

As your team engages the innovation process, your work together invites each team member's unique perspectives and stories, inspires new questions, and encourages everyone to offer their own innovative ideas. This process shifts the youth leader's role from being the sole idea generator to the idea-cultivator. Everyone is invited to think innovatively together!

Create a youth ministry that is no longer "mine" but "ours."

Focus your priorities where teenagers need you most

Perhaps one of the greatest challenges for youth leaders is not having youth ministry priorities, but determining which of these priorities gets your attention. You cannot do it all, nor should you. So how do you determine where to invest your time and resources? What rubric do you use? Implementing Sticky Faith Innovation gives you the tools to discern and start addressing the most pressing needs of your teenagers.

Your shift toward a Sticky Faith Innovation posture empowers you to identify and set your priorities with confidence.

Include and inspire others with clear communication

Once you know your priorities, you can communicate them with interested parents, volunteers, and church leadership. Sometimes invested adults may seem aloof, anxious, or even angry over some of your ministry decisions. It's easy to blame them for overreacting, but at times, clearer communication about where you're taking the ministry is all that's needed.

Your Sticky Faith Innovation posture empowers you to clearly and effectively communicate the youth ministry's direction with confidence, building trust with your leaders and parents.

For example, as we've mentioned throughout this book, sharing your gap sentence with those in your church clearly captures what you're doing and why you're doing it:

Because our teenagers feel/believe "_____
_____ "

" [current answer]

We will innovate _____
[selected program area or practice]

In order that young people might believe/discover "_____
_____ "

[Jesus-centered answer].

The Sticky Faith Innovation process does more than help you generate new ideas. Your innovative work inspires everyone to unleash their compassion, creativity, and courage. You're making space for volunteers' contributions, focusing your efforts on where teenagers need you most, and communicating your goals with others in ways that might inspire them to join you. More are included and fewer are left in the dark. Everyone is inspired to see God at work.

Unleashing the congregation's compassion, creativity, and courage

In our research, we've noticed that Sticky Faith Innovation can have an enormously positive ripple effect. When leaders like you invested in the Sticky Faith Innovation process, many shared it with their senior pastors, which led to the whole church engaging in innovation together. For example, one leader told us,

After going through this innovation process, I shared it with my senior pastor. He loved it. He and I then led our church leadership through this innovation process and came up with a four-year plan for our entire church to better engage our community. I've also used this process to reimagine small groups and family ministry. —Martin, youth leader

Sticky Faith Innovation can help move your whole church from stuck to sticky, unleashing all generations' compassion, creativity, and courage to step into the spaces of young people's—and the world's—greatest needs.

Innovating around Sticky Faith principles

Every attempt at Sticky Faith Innovation is another opportunity to make your youth ministry approaches more effective. In fact, the more you innovate, the more you'll find new gaps where your students need you.

As you look for inspiration for future innovation, don't forget the findings from our original Sticky Faith research. You can catalyze your youth ministry's effectiveness with these already-essential Sticky Faith principles:

- intergenerational relationships

- a gospel that grows with them

- partnership with families

- room for doubt and questions

- more thoughtful engagement in justice and service

Sticky Faith Innovation can help you create new and effective ways to lean into these scaffolds to support your teenagers' lasting faith.

Intergenerational relationships

We've learned from our original Sticky Faith research that while teenagers value their peer friendships, they also benefit from intergenerational relationships. Many churches have responded to this finding, attempting to get young and old to share more experiences together. These have included whole church gatherings, dinners, mission trips, shared hobbies, and outings. Since then, we've learned that the intergenerational challenges congregations face are not in pulling off events but in actually generating interaction between young and old. Young people tell us how they do not know how to engage adults and feel intimidated. Similarly, adults admit feeling ignorant of younger generations' interests, language, or technology, and are equally anxious!

A practical way that our Sticky Faith research framed intergenerational relationships was by emphasizing the importance of flipping the typical teenager-to-adult support ratio of five teenagers to one adult by instead imagining five adults invested in each teenager. Teenagers need unconditional love beyond their parents, in trusted relationships with adults like grandparents, mentors, teachers, coaches, pastors, and youth leaders. This 5:1 ratio symbolizes that teenagers feel supported in their faith when they perceive that there are at least five adults in their lives who care for them, with no strings attached.

Innovation can help create a culture that provides new opportunities for young and old to learn and interact with each other. Your innovative work may inspire you to get feedback from your teenagers who have experienced intergenerational support. You could also gather adults who see themselves as one of a teenager's "five" and ask them about their experiences, hopes, and needs. This kind of listening may lead you to innovate new programs or practices that better support adults who want to support teenagers.

Consider this:

- Run a Sticky Faith Innovation process with your teenagers, specifically asking them about the adult support they have or desire. Innovate to provide more adult support for your teenagers.

- Run an innovation process with adults in your community, specifically asking them how they are already supporting and might better support young people. Innovate to provide education, training, or opportunities to be one of those five supporting adults.

Sticky gospel (good news that grows with them)

Too many young people we talk with admit that they've "grown out" of their childhood faith. Our original Sticky Faith research points to the idea that as young people grow up, they start to feel relationally distant from the God they were introduced to when they were younger. They long for a trusting relationship with a good God who knows them now, can empathize with them today, and can speak to their instabilities in a practical way. Sticky Faith Innovation can help your whole church develop new perspectives and ways to teach, demonstrate, and live out the gospel's good news, giving teenagers renewed hope that they can trust a God who is still near and for them no matter how fast their lives are changing.

Consider this:

- Beyond conversion stories, how might you tell faith stories that include themes of trust, failure, lament, hope, unknowns, or wonder?

- How might you run an innovation process where the good news of the gospel is paired with a topic that teenagers care deeply about—like relationships, careers, talents, the environment, or justice—to expand your youth ministry's vision of the gospel?

Partnership with families

Youth leaders are great at reminding parents that parents are the primary disciplers of their children. In fact, research—

including our original Sticky Faith research—has named the significant impact parents have on their kids' faith.

What youth leaders do not always do as well is provide resources to help parents and guardians succeed. Sticky Faith Innovation has the potential to provide ways for you to work with parents, learn about their own needs, and innovate the kinds of resources and support that may be most helpful for them. Applying the Sticky Faith Innovation process to the ways you work with parents takes the guessing out of what they need and activates real steps toward supporting them. You develop a culture that works *with* parents and guardians rather than without (or even against!) them.

Consider this:

- Run an innovation process for parents of 8th graders or 11th graders, inviting them to talk about their hopes and fears as parents of kids who are about to attend high school or graduate to their next stage in life. How might your team come up with creative ways to support these parents during this transition?

- Instead of holding a regular parent meeting, try a shortened Sticky Faith Innovation process that lets parents try to solve a parenting challenge like sharing a family meal, talking about sex, discussing technology, or bringing up dating.

A safe place to doubt and explore

Our original Sticky Faith research also recognized that teenagers need safe spaces to express their doubts about faith. Most young people say they experience doubt over faith and religious topics, but few share their concerns or questions with others. Students need safe spaces and trusted relationships to express and work out their faith.

While many youth leaders agree with these findings, some find them hard to address as their church culture is unprepared and unsure about how to hold doubt and questions. Sticky Faith Innovation can inspire leaders to find new ways to support teenagers as they experience, express, and work through their questions. Imagine pulling together a cross-section of church leaders, parents, and teenagers to listen to young peoples' stories, questions, hopes, and disappointments.

Consider this:

- Run an innovation process with your students, asking them about their faith and doubt. Discover what's really concerning them, and then brainstorm ways to make sharing doubt a normal part of your youth ministry and the life of faith.

- Run an innovation process where your students try to understand their friends' quests for identity, belonging, and purpose. What doubts might they have? What good news might God want to invite them toward?

Sticky Faith and justice

Our original Sticky Faith research pointed to the reality that many of our church's conceptions of justice are too narrow. Embedded in Sticky Faith Innovation is a call to a simple yet profound shift—that innovation teaches us to look outward. Our starting points do not originate from our assumptions or even our cultural traditions. They start with the people we serve fueled by the gospel that claims that God loves the whole world. God's love calls for justice where the most vulnerable in our society are seen and cared for by God's people. Sticky Faith Innovation's vision does not (and cannot) stop with serving our own teenagers. Its justice orientation helps us see more teenagers in our communities and calls us to play our part to advocate for them as local and global neighbors.

Imagine what would happen if churches started listening to teachers, government officials, prison guards, mental health experts, nurses, and diverse faith leaders. Might innovation provide new visions for how we can serve more teenagers and their worlds? We believe so.

Consider this:

- Run an innovation process in which you only listen to teenagers who don't go to church. Discover their needs, so your youth ministry can better serve them, regardless of whether they ever choose to join your church.

- Run an innovation process with your teenagers where they empathize with an underresourced or marginalized group in your community and creatively come up with ways of serving and empowering the most vulnerable in the city. Then, collaborate with community partners, teenagers, and those you seek to serve to make it happen.

You

The stories and reflections of youth leaders like Trevor, Anna, Irene, Miguel, Damon, and Haley give us so much hope. But we need you to know something: they're just like you. And you're inspiring, just like them.

Youth ministry's most precious gifts are the people like you who feel called to serve young people. You've gone all-in to give all you've got.

You are our heroes.

Currently, as we are writing about our Sticky Faith Innovation research, COVID-19 has uprooted the world to the point where many ministry leaders feel there is no "going back to normal." In addition, our cities ache as racism, injustice, oppression, and death go unheard and unaddressed. The gaps between our country's current answers and the hope of Jesus-centered answers are painfully deep and wide.

You're called into this gap.

You have also joined a remarkable youth ministry lineage of others who have given their lives to stand in the gap to better teenagers' lives. The beauty and the challenge now rest with you to push forward and to make the necessary moves to see and serve today's teenagers and their journeys of life and faith.

 If you would like a seasoned guide or coach on this innovation journey, check out stickyfaithinnovation.com/**training** for opportunities to gain additional support from the FYI team. We'd love to walk with you every step of the way.

May your compassion increase.
May your creativity overflow.
May your courage soar.
May your own steps of faith inspire theirs.
May you fearlessly stand in the gap.
And may you know that, through the gospel of
Jesus, there is hope for every teenager and good
news for the whole world.
Grace and peace.

REFLECT

1. What steps have you taken already to move your ministry from being "yours" to "ours"? What future steps do you want to take to further live into this vision of shared leadership in your youth ministry?

REFLECT

2. Of the Sticky Faith principles we describe in this chapter, which one is your youth ministry currently doing well? Which one might be worth improving through another round of Sticky Faith Innovation?

REFLECT

3. How might Sticky Faith Innovation be inspiring you to serve young people beyond your church? Who are the teenagers that need the compassion, creativity, and courage your youth ministry and church possess? How might you stand in the gap with these teenagers through God's empowerment and grace?

Appendix
Sticky Faith Innovation
Research Project Overview

The Sticky Faith Innovation body of research, originally named the Youth Ministry Innovations (YMI) project, was conducted by the Fuller Youth Institute from 2016–2019. This appendix provides an *abbreviated description* of the research method and procedures.

Based on extensive preliminary work and literature review, the YMI research team identified the primary goal of the project as addressing the undermet needs of teenagers by generating innovative ideas that are forged through collaborative relationships and piloted in participating congregations. This aim was operationalized through primary and secondary research objectives.

Primary Objective: To develop both innovative approaches and innovative leaders that support adolescents in the spaces where they need the most support from the church, but where the church often feels the least equipped to help. Our framework incorporated Christian practices and practical theology with a variety of innovation methods (such as design thinking).

Secondary Objectives: First, to create and test practices that become reproducible resources that will benefit youth ministry leaders and young people. Second, to create and test a process for innovation that can be learned and implemented by leaders so they can create their own innovative practices that meet the unique needs of their young people.

Sticky Faith Innovation research cohorts

To address these objectives, we conducted three one-year cohorts. These cohorts served our team by giving us multiple rounds of feedback, allowing us to adjust training and progressively refine our innovation model. By the end of the project, we worked with 51 churches[29] and more than 100 youth leaders across the United States (see the list of participating churches below). Our examples for this book draw from the experiences of these youth leaders and churches. Through another research project called Ministry Innovations with Young Adults (funded by Lilly Endowment Inc.), an additional 43 churches and nearly 200 young adults and church leaders helped refine our innovation model. Stay tuned for forthcoming resources.

Prior to commencing the YMI cohorts, we hosted pilot gatherings to test our approach and to receive crucial feedback from diverse, influential youth ministry leaders from across the country. Across the three cohorts, we selected youth ministries and leaders who self-identified as having the time to invest in the cohort and a context ready for change. Churches were also selected to increase representation regarding denomination, church size, socioeconomic status, race, and location (i.e., urban, suburban, and rural; region of the United States). Each participating church team consisted of two youth leaders: a point person and a ministry partner. As described in our innovation process, these leaders developed an innovation team and a discernment team to share their work with a broader set of leaders.

Ten out of the 51 churches applied and participated for a second cohort year. These churches' extended participation allowed us to learn from their work as it unfolded over a longer time horizon. Six out the 51 churches, due to a variety of circumstances (church leadership turnover, church crises, shifts in church priorities, etc.), withdrew from the cohort prior to the one-year mark.

The YMI research team trained participating church leaders through an online learning platform, a three-day innovation summit, and monthly coaching. The final cohort event required all leaders to share their innovative new approaches with one another, including what they learned, what they would do differently, what they would recommend to other churches, and what they plan to do next as a result of their learning. Further, final reports were written by ministry point leaders, describing their process, impressions, challenges, and successes. These self-assessments, along with leader pre- and post-assessments and coaches' feedback, provided us thicker descriptions of youth leaders' thinking, challenges, stories, and breakthroughs.

Participant pre- and post-assessments

We conducted program evaluations through voluntary pre- and post-assessments with teenagers from participating youth ministries. We distributed these surveys through the help of YMI youth leaders. Data from these surveys allowed us to assess the impact of new ministry approaches on participating teenagers and identify any specific changes in teenagers' self-perceptions of their identity, belonging, and purpose.

Assessments included questions evaluating young people's identity, belonging, and purpose. Each young person was asked to provide five words or phrases to describe their identity, belonging, and purpose (e.g., "If you were to ask yourself, 'Who am I?' how would you answer this question using five different words or short phrases?"). Participants were then asked questions about their responses to these open-ended questions (e.g., "How satisfied are you with your current responses to the question, 'Who am I?'").

Across all three cohorts, 1,160 adolescents completed the pre-assessment, 770 completed the post-assessment, and 308 of these individuals completed both pre- and post-assessments. Post-assessment results indicate that participants' experiences in the new forms of ministry produced strong growth in their relationships with God. Of the sample, 85.1 percent indicated that they grew in their relationship with God moderately to dramatically. A strong majority of participants (81.7 percent) indicated they hope to continue engaging in their youth ministry's new approach, and a majority (60.5 percent) of post-assessment participants shared about their experience with non-practice participants, likely indicating enthusiasm for the new approach.

Of those who completed both pre- and post-assessments, there was a statistically significant increase in teenagers' 1) satisfaction with their current responses to the question of "Who am I?", 2) degree of exploration related to the question of "Who am I?", 3) sense that they are able to exert personal influence in their church, 4) satisfaction with their current response to the question of "What difference do I make in the world?", 5) sense of purpose in the world, and 6) sense that their choices in life were shaped by that purpose. We also found a statistically significant increase in participants' comfortability with sharing their deepest pains, anxieties, and losses with others.

Analyses of open-ended identity, belonging, and purpose questions were conducted using Linguistic Inquiry and Word Count (LIWC) software. Analyses revealed that participants tended to use positive emotions to describe their identity and purpose (e.g., "funny", "optimistic", "loving", "kind") and rarely used negative emotions in their responses. Young people also often defined their identity, belonging, and purpose using social words.

Participating Sticky Faith Innovation research churches

Over 13 denominations were represented, in addition to 8 congregations claiming no denominational affiliation. The largest traditions represented were Presbyterian (11), United Methodist (7), Evangelical Covenant (4), and Lutheran (4). Churches ranged in size of active congregational participants, including approximately 99 or fewer (2 percent of churches), 100–249 (18 percent of churches), 250–499 (21 percent of churches), 500–999 (10 percent of churches), 1,000–2,999 (39 percent of churches), over 3,000 (10 percent of churches). Youth ministries ranged in size of active student participants, including approximately 10 or fewer (2 percent of youth ministries), 10–24 (31 percent of youth ministries), 25–49 (14 percent of youth ministries), 50–149 (28 percent of youth ministries), over 150 (25 percent of youth ministries). In terms of census regions of the US, they were distributed among the Midwest (37 percent), West (33 percent), South (22 percent), and Northeast (8 percent). In terms of racial diversity (based on reporting churches), 73 percent of youth ministries identified as "mostly White," 17 percent were "multiracial," 8 percent were "mostly Asian," and 2 percent were "mostly Black or African American."

For further analysis of data, see:

Steven C. Argue, Caleb W. Roose, and Tyler S. Greenway, "Identity, belonging, and purpose as lenses for empathizing with adolescents," *Journal of Youth Ministry* 18, no. 1 (Spring 2020): 74–87

Steven C. Argue, Caleb W. Roose, and Tyler S. Greenway, "Forming youth through engagement in holistic Christian practices," (Paper presented at the Association of Youth Ministry Educators Annual Conference, Minneapolis, MN, October 2019)

The following churches participated in the Youth Ministry Innovations (i.e., Sticky Faith Innovation) research cohorts:

Arlington Countryside Church, Arlington Heights, IL

Ascent Community Church, Louisville, CO

Bellevue Presbyterian Church, Bellevue, WA

Beulah Presbyterian Church, Pittsburgh, PA

Calvary Church Los Gatos, Los Gatos, CA

Carmichael Seventh-day Adventist Church, Sacramento, CA

Christ Church of Oak Brook, Oak Brook, IL

Christ Presbyterian Church, Edina, MN

Colonial Church, Edina, MN

Crossroads African Methodist Episcopal Church, Indianapolis, IN

Eagle Rock Baptist Church, Eagle Rock, CA

Faith Lutheran Church, Glen Ellyn, IL

Fellowship Memphis, Memphis, TN

Fellowship Monrovia, Monrovia, CA

First Baptist Church Albemarle, Albemarle, NC

First Covenant Church of Oakland, Oakland, CA

First Presbyterian Church, Colorado Springs, CO

First Presbyterian Church, Nashville, TN

First Presbyterian Church, Spokane, WA

First United Methodist Church of Little Rock, Little Rock, AR

Frontline Community Church, Grand Rapids, MI

Grace Pasadena Church, Pasadena, CA

Granger Community Church, Granger, IN

Hamilton Mill United Methodist Church, Dacula, GA

Harrisburg United Methodist Church, Harrisburg, NC

Heritage Church, Rock Island, IL

Hosanna! Lutheran Church, Lakeville, MN

John Knox Presbyterian Church, North Olmsted, OH

Knox Presbyterian Church, Ann Arbor, MI

Lake Grove Presbyterian Church, Lake Oswego, OR

Lutheran Church of the Atonement, Barrington, IL

Mars Hill Bible Church, Grand Rapids, MI

New Community Covenant Church, Chicago, IL

New Covenant Church, Winter Springs, FL

New Song Church, Santa Ana, CA

Nexus Church, Portland, OR

Peachtree Road United Methodist Church, Atlanta, GA

Placerville Seventh-day Adventist Church, Placerville, CA

Port City Community Church, Wilmington, NC

Princeton Alliance Church, Plainsboro, NJ

Providence United Methodist Church, Mt. Juliet, TN

Quest Church, Seattle, WA

Rock Spring United Methodist Church, Rock Spring, GA

Simi Covenant Church, Simi Valley, CA

St. John's Lutheran Church, Phoenix, MD

Summit Church, Orlando, FL

The Garden Fellowship, Chatsworth, CA

Third Reformed Church, Pella, IA

Trinity Presbyterian Church, Atlanta, GA

Trinity Presbyterian Church, Woodbury, MN

Willowdale Chapel, Kennett Square, PA

Assumptions and limitations

While the research team made every effort to ensure an academically rigorous process, no research project is without assumptions and limitations.

Our context as researchers. The Fuller Youth Institute is located within Fuller Theological Seminary, one of the most influential evangelical institutions and the largest multidenominational seminary. While Fuller identifies as evangelical, it serves students nationally and internationally who hold a diversity of denominational commitments and cultural backgrounds. We recognize that Fuller's location in Southern California provides unique opportunities and challenges for participating churches, as local churches may perceive working with FYI to be more accessible than those who are from other parts of the country. Further, our own social locations (our research team was predominantly White and highly educated, and the authors of this book are both male) and ministry experiences have, no doubt, shaped our approaches and assessments.

Participating youth leaders and churches. The majority of participating churches in our research had resources to employ either part-time or full-time paid youth workers who served as the point leaders on their innovation teams. To counterbalance this bias toward paid youth workers, we listened closely to their ministry partners, the majority of whom were volunteers, and continually adjusted our training to accommodate a broader scope of youth leaders. Further, while we sought to work with a diverse range of churches, we also recognize that the term "innovation" itself comes with cultural assumptions about how one collaborates and implements new ministry approaches. The feedback we collected throughout the cohort allowed us to make iterative adjustments with every cohort to contextualize innovation for a variety of ministry contexts. Additionally, the ethnic, racial, and socioeconomic diversity of participating churches could have been increased to be more representative of the demographics of the United States. Subsequent FYI research projects correct this imbalance to be more fully representative.

Assessing innovative change. In this book, we have focused primarily on the stories of leaders who succeeded with their innovations and learned from their innovative attempts within the timeframe of the one-year cohorts. Some innovative attempts did not result in immediate success and only gained momentum after the conclusion of the cohorts. Others did not succeed, but nevertheless helped leaders learn more about the necessary conditions for change in their churches and youth ministries. We recognize that approaches to change vary depending on the youth ministry context and that some trial and error is a part of the innovation process. Hence, interpreting "success" and evaluating "change" varies with each ministry.

Student feedback. Our assessment of teenagers' experiences relied heavily on youth leaders administering the surveys developed by our FYI team. Survey response rates varied from church to church, with findings articulating some meta-themes, yet also revealing the opportunity for more assessment that could have come from focus groups or site visits for even thicker descriptions. See Kara Powell and Brad Griffin's book 3 *Big Questions that Change Every Teenager: Making the Most of Your Conversations and Connections* for a deeper dive into the lives of today's teenagers.

Our theological commitments. Last, but certainly not least, the Fuller Youth Institute (as part of Fuller Theological Seminary) holds particular beliefs and theological commitments that have grounded and guided our research. Undoubtedly, these commitments have influenced the research in ways that those from other traditions may find unhelpful.

STICKY FAITH **INNOVATION**

About the Authors

Steven Argue, PhD, is an associate professor of youth, family, and culture at Fuller Theological Seminary and the applied research strategist at the Fuller Youth Institute (FYI). He has taught undergraduate and graduate youth ministry courses for over a decade, worked in multiple ministry contexts including the lead pastoral team at Mars Hill Bible Church (Grand Rapids, MI), and serves on the board for the Association of Youth Ministry Educators. He researches, speaks, and writes regularly on topics surrounding adolescence, emerging adulthood, faith, and spiritual struggle. He has coauthored two books: *Growing With: Every Parent's Guide to Helping Teenagers and Young Adults Thrive in Their Faith, Family, and Future* (Baker Books, 2019); and *18 Plus: Parenting Your Emerging Adults* (Orange, 2018). Steve and his wife, Jen, live in Southern California and love being parents to Kara, Elise, and Lauren. Twitter: @stevenargue

Caleb Roose is a project manager at the Fuller Youth Institute (FYI), where he advises and facilitates FYI church trainings and research, coaches and consults with churches around the country, and develops resources. He is a graduate student at Fuller Theological Seminary (Master of Divinity) and has a Bachelor of Arts in Biblical Studies and Theology from Biola University and the Torrey Honors Institute. Caleb is passionate about helping young people wrestle with their faith and encouraging leaders to do the same. He has worked in a variety of ministry and professional roles, including volunteering in youth ministries, serving as an associate pastor of discipleship and administration, counseling at and running youth camps, ministering in six different countries with Youth With a Mission (YWAM), and managing an after-school program for kids. A Southern California native, Caleb lives 30 minutes from his hometown with his wife, Colleen, and two young daughters, Lilah and Eliana. Twitter: @CalebRoose

ACKNOWLEDGMENTS

Innovative ideas rarely originate with solitary genius. Instead, the best ideas emerge from everyday conversations with real people facing real challenges wanting to make a real difference—together.

That's why Sticky Faith Innovation is so special to us.

This book is the fruit of intense meetings, countless emails, colorful whiteboards, revamped trainings, moving stories, and surprising breakthroughs—all shared with some of the most remarkable people we know. While acknowledging them hardly does justice to our gratitude, we recognize each person's significant contribution to this resource and their commitment to youth leaders and young people.

We are especially indebted to our Sticky Faith Innovation research teammates at the Fuller Youth Institute (FYI), Kara Powell, Brad Griffin, and colleague Scott Cormode, the Hugh DePree Professor of Leadership at Fuller Seminary. Their tireless wisdom, encouragement, challenge, grace, and optimism have kept us going and clarified our message throughout the project.

FYI also has an amazingly talented team who selflessly invested their time and skills to make this book possible and come alive—Macy Davis, Rachel Dodd, Zachariah Ellis, Tyler Greenway, Jennifer Guerra Aldana, Jenica Halula, Jennifer Hananouchi, Roslyn Hernández, Jane Hong-Guzman de Leon, Andy Jung, Yulee Lee, Jake Mulder, Giovanny Panginda, and Katherine Whitaker.

The valuable contributions of FYI's research and project assistants, including Laura Atwater, Emily Colledge, Abbey Craigg, Cassandra Curry, Rudy Estrada, Patrick Jacques, and Greg Kilpatrick contributed to the depth and care of this research and the leaders this project served.

We also benefited from the investment and input from voices outside FYI as well. Proven leaders like April Diaz and Mike Park served as coaches for our Sticky Faith Innovation research cohorts and as perpetual conversation partners. The strategic feedback of our advisory team—including Kristen Ivy, Mark Oestreicher, Martin Saunders, and Andrew Zirschky—made our work sharper and more helpful for youth leaders with their every suggestion and insight.

This book was also fine-tuned by leaders who gave honest and insightful feedback on our manuscript. Thank you Lauren Argue, Grace Cowen, Daniel Kim, Young-Ki Kim, Kyle Lake, Jeremy Morelock, Katie Peterson, and Emily Wickstrom.

Our four years of research were made possible by those willing to invest in this project's vision. We are grateful to Lilly Endowment Inc. and Sacred Harvest Foundation for their investment and belief in the Fuller Youth Institute's mission.

To our spouses—Jen and Colleen—life and faith are more meaningful and exciting because they're shared with you. Your impromptu conversations, writer's block encouragements, and dedicated interest have made this book, and us, better.

Research and theory are of little use without acting on them. That's why we honor the hundreds of youth leaders who have engaged in our Sticky Faith Innovation research cohorts, risking new ideas to serve their young people. This book would not exist without your stories of compassion, creativity, and courage. Thank you.

ENDNOTES

[1]A. W. Geiger and Leslie Davis, "A growing number of American teenagers—particularly girls—are facing depression," *Pew Research Center* (July 12, 2019), https://www.pewresearch.org/fact-tank/2019/07/12/a-growing-number-of-american-teenagers-particularly-girls-are-facing-depression.

[2] Nikki Graf, "A majority of U.S. teens fear a shooting could happen at their school, and most parents share their concern," *Pew Research Center* (April 8, 2018), https://www.pewresearch.org/fact-tank/2018/04/18/a-majority-of-u-s-teens-fear-a-shooting-could-happen-at-their-school-and-most-parents-share-their-concern.

Drew DeSilver, "The concerns and challenges of being a U.S. teen: What the data show," *Pew Research Center* (February 26, 2019), https://www.pewresearch.org/fact-tank/2019/02/26/the-concerns-and-challenges-of-being-a-u-s-teen-what-the-data-show.

[3]DeSilver, "The concerns and challenges of being a U.S. teen."

[4]Steven C. Argue, Caleb W. Roose, and Tyler S. Greenway, "Identity, belonging, and purpose as lenses for empathizing with adolescents," *Journal of Youth Ministry* 18, no. 1 (Spring 2020): 74–87.

[5]See the Appendix for the list of participating churches.

[6]Mark Lau Branson and Juan Francisco Martínez, *Churches, Cultures & Leadership: A Practical Theology of Congregations and Ethnicities* (Downers Grove, IL: IVP Academic, 2011), http://public.eblib.com/choice/publicfullrecord.aspx?p=2007059.

[7]Design thinking "is a process for creative problem solving" in many different industries. IDEO, "What Is Design Thinking?," *IDEO U* blog (accessed July 29, 2020), https://www.ideou.com/blogs/inspiration/what-is-design-thinking. Our team has also learned from the following resources:

Matthew Ridenour, "IDEO Consultation" (consultation, Fuller Theological seminary, December 6, 2016);

IDEO, *The Field Guide to Human-Centered Design: Design Kit* (San Francisco: IDEO, 2015);

Tom Kelley and David Kelley, *Creative Confidence: Unleashing the Creative Potential Within Us All* (New York: Crown Business, 2013);

Jake Knapp, John Zeratsky, and Braden Kowitz, *Sprint: How to Solve Big Problems and Test New Ideas in Just Five Days* (New York: Simon & Schuster, 2016).

[8]In our Growing Young research, we discovered that empathizing with young people today is one of six essential strategies for creating churches young people love. In our Sticky Faith Innovation research, we've also discovered that empathy is the launchpad for innovation. We must understand who we seek to serve. See Kara Eckmann Powell, Jake Mulder, and Brad Griffin, *Growing Young: Six Essential Strategies to Help Young People Discover and Love Your Church* (Grand Rapids, MI: Baker Books, 2016), 88–125.

9For the majority of quotations shared throughout this book, we have supplied pseudonyms and edited some quotations slightly for clarity.

10Generational theory (espousing 20-year generational cycles) was popularized by the work of Neil Howe and William Strauss, *Millennials Rising: The Next Great Generation*, 3rd ed. (New York: Vintage, 2000). The length of such generational cohorts has been challenged with the emergence of Generation Z due to the speed in which society is changing. See Jean M. Twenge, *iGen: Why Today's Super-Connected Kids Are Growing Up Less Rebellious, More Tolerant, Less Happy—and Completely Unprepared for Adulthood—and What That Means for the Rest of Us*, 2nd ed. (New York: Atria Books, 2017), 40–57.

11This concept is masterfully identified and developed in Hartmut Rosa, *Alienation and Acceleration: Towards a Critical Theory of Late-Modern Temporality* (Summertalk) (Aarhus, Denmark: Aarhus University Press, 2010).

12Kate Murphy, "You're Not Listening. Here's Why," *New York Times* (February 11, 2020), https://www.nytimes.com/2020/02/11/well/family/listening-relationships-marriage-closeness-communication-bias.html.

13See Chap Clark, *Hurt 2.0: Inside the World of Today's Teenagers (Youth, Family, and Culture)* (Grand Rapids, MI: Baker Academic, 2011), 43–45. Also, in Kara Eckmann Powell and Chap Clark, *Sticky Faith: Everyday Ideas to Build Lasting Faith in Your Kids* (Grand Rapids, MI: Zondervan, 2011), 13–30. Note that while 70 percent of teenagers experience doubts, only half tell anyone about them.

14Kenda Creasy Dean, *Practicing Passion: Youth and the Quest for a Passionate Church* (Grand Rapids, MI: Eerdmans, 2004), 29–53.

15Steven C. Argue and Tyler S. Greenway, "Empathy with Emerging Generations as a Foundation for Ministry," *Christian Education Journal* 17, no. 1 (2020), 110–29. https://doi.org/10.1177/0739891319899666.

16Brené Brown, *Daring Greatly* (New York: Penguin, 2012), 81.

17Two examples include the Gospel writers' accounts of Jesus saying very little, but his actions were laced with symbolism that drew on Israel's narrative. The religious leaders' response was one of outrage (cf. Mark 11:18 and 14:1; Luke 19:47; John 5:18 and 7:1). Also, Jesus' encounter with the woman at the well is a beautiful scene where she runs to tell others to "come, see a man who told me everything I ever did" (John 4:29). It is unlikely that Jesus told her "everything," but this is how she felt. She felt known and understood. This is empathy.

18Some of these questions overlap with the interview protocol used for FYI's research with teenagers featured in *3 Big Questions that Change Every Teenager.* To access over 300 questions you can ask young people, see Kara Eckmann Powell and Brad M. Griffin, *3 Big Questions that Change Every Teenager: Making the Most of Your Conversations and Connections* (Baker, 2021).

[19]Powell and Griffin, *3 Big Questions that Change Every Teenager*. This resource expands upon this listening completed by Sticky Faith Innovation youth leaders through an extensive interview process conducted by the FYI team. Find out more about this and other resources at fulleryouthinstitute. org.

[20]Our colleague Scott Cormode (who is a theology and leadership professor and expert on innovation) highlights that while expanding, "quantity" is more important than "quality." He offers an example—a study in which two groups created pottery. In Group 1, students were given clay and instructed to make the best art they could within a designated time period. In Group 2, students were given unlimited clay and told to generate as many art pieces they could within that same time period. To summarize, Group 1 was told to focus on quality, and Group 2 was told to focus on quantity. When the two groups' work was compared, Group 2 actually produced more creative, quality pieces. Focusing on quantity beats focusing on quality. See also: Scott Cormode, *The Innovative Church: How Leaders and Their Congregations Can Adapt in an Ever-Changing World* (Grand Rapids, MI: Baker Academic, 2020), 135–136.

[21]For more resources on Asset-Based Community Development (ABCD), see resources like the "Tool Kit" developed by DePaul University. Asset-Based Community Development Institute, "Resources," DePaul University, accessed September 22, 2020, https://resources.depaul.edu/abcd-institute/resources.

[22]Kara E. Powell, Brad M. Griffin, and Cheryl A. Crawford, *Sticky Faith, Youth Worker Edition: Practical Ideas to Nurture Long-term Faith in Teenagers* (Grand Rapids, MI: Zondervan, 2011), 11–25.

[23]Caleb W. Roose, Tyler S. Greenway, and Steven C. Argue, "Forming Youth through Engagement in Holistic Christian Practices" (paper presented at the Association of Youth Ministry Educators Annual Conference, Minneapolis, MN, September, 2019).

[24]"Pictaphone," Stumingames, October 15, 2013, http://stumingames. com/2013/10/pictaphone-stumin.

[25]Chauncey Wilson, "Using Brainwriting for Rapid Idea Generation," *Smashing Magazine* blog (December 16, 2013), https://www.smashingmagazine. com/2013/12/using-brainwriting-for-rapid-idea-generation.

[26]Miss Chatz, "How to Storyboard: A Basic Guide for Aspiring Artists," *Design & Illustration Envato Tuts+* blog (May 30, 2018), https://design.tutsplus.com/ articles/how-to-storyboard-basic-guides-for-aspiring-artists--cms-30962.

[27]Powell, Griffin, and Crawford, *Sticky Faith, Youth Worker Edition*.

[28]Powell, Griffin, and Crawford, *Sticky Faith, Youth Worker Edition*.

[29]This total number excludes the few churches who withdrew from the cohort within the first 90 days.

All churches
grow old.
But strategic
churches are
growing young.

Packed with ideas based on groundbreaking research with over 250 of the nation's leading congregations, *Growing Young* shows you how to position your church to reach younger generations in a way that breathes life into the whole church.

Find resources that can help your church start growing young at
fulleryouthinstitute.org/**growingyoung**.

Today's young people are anxious.
Teach them they're not alone.

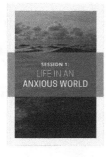

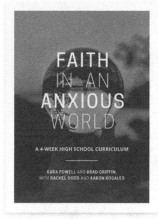

SESSION 1:
LIFE IN AN
ANXIOUS WORLD

SESSION 2:
LIFE IN A
RELATIONAL WORLD

FAITH IN AN ANXIOUS WORLD

A 4-WEEK HIGH SCHOOL CURRICULUM

KARA POWELL AND BRAD GRIFFIN,
WITH RACHEL DODD AND AARON ROSALES

SESSION 3:
LIFE IN A
HURTING WORLD

SESSION 4:
LIFE IN A
HOPEFUL WORLD

Faith in an Anxious World is a 4-week research-based multimedia curriculum that will equip you with the tools you need to guide young people in your care, linking anxiety and depression with conversations about discipleship and faithful living. Together you'll reflect on New Testament stories, watch Jesus enter into anxious situations, and explore life in an anxious but hope-filled world.

Download a free sample and find out more at
fulleryouthinstitute.org/**anxiousworld**.

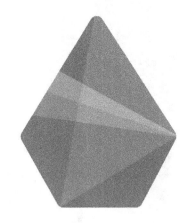

FULLER YOUTH

INSTITUTE

WE TURN RESEARCH
INTO PRACTICAL RESOURCES,
EQUIPPING LEADERS AND
PARENTS TO HELP
**FAITHFUL YOUNG PEOPLE
CHANGE OUR WORLD.**

Find more resources for your ministry at
fulleryouthinstitute.org.

STICKY FAITH **INNOVATION**

CPSIA information can be obtained
at www.ICGtesting.com
Printed in the USA
LVHW010027150121
676462LV00005B/735

9 780991 488087